Dancing Forever with Spirit

Astonishing Insights from Heaven

by

Garnet Schulhauser

For permission, serialization, condensation, adaptions, or for our catalog of other publications, write to Ozark Mountain Publishing, Inc., P.O. box 754, Huntsville, AR 72740, ATTN: Permissions Department.

Library of Congress Cataloging-in-Publication Data

Schulhauser, Garnet, 1951 -

Dancing Forever with Spirit by Garnet Schulhauser

A chance meeting with a homeless man marks the beginning of enlightening and soul searching conversations with Garnet's Spirit Guide answering all of the probing questions we all want to know about life here as well as the hereafter.

1. Spirit Guides 2. Reincarnation 3. Life After Death

I. Schulhauser, Garnet, 1951 – II. Reincarnation III. Metaphysics IV. Title

Library of Congress Catalog Card Number: 2015933166

ISBN: 9781940265070

Cover Design: noir33.com

Book set in: Calibri Light and Gabriola

Book Design: Tab Pillar

Published by:

PO Box 754

Huntsville, AR 72740

800-935-0045 or 479-738-2348 fax: 479-738-2448

WWW.OZARKMT.COM

Printed in the United States of America

Endorsements

"Garnet Schulhauser offers a brilliant account of our spiritual nature from the perspective of Albert, his delightful spirit guide. This book allows us to travel vicariously with Garnet when Albert takes him on journeys to the Hall of Records, other planets and past civilizations. During these travels, Albert makes us privy to valuable knowledge about the life of Jesus, the Source, and the role of the Council of Wise Ones and aliens in creating a new Earth. This books is a must read for anyone seeking to understand their life purpose and to evolve."

Kathryn Andries – author of *Soul Choices: Six Paths to Fulfilling Relationships, Naked in Public: Dream Symbols Revealed, The Dream Doctor,* and *Soul Choices: Six Paths to Find Your Life Purpose*

"Garnet Schulhauser has done it once again with the writings of *Dancing Forever with Spirit.* I am truly grateful that Garnet asked the questions of his soul and allowed the most unpredictable situation to guide him to the answers. *Dancing on a Stamp* was the first recording of Garnet and Albert's journey; four pages into the book, I was hooked, and left wanting more. *Dancing Forever with Spirit* is that more, more answers, more understanding, more guidance, and it leaves you ready for more. I opened this book and literally could not put it down until I turned the last page. Thank you, Garnet, for being the voice and allowing Albert to show you and all of us, why we are here and what this life is all about."

"In the Sovereignty of The Mind is Birthed The Divinity of The Soul" – **Rev. Brenda Braden**

"Warning! Reading this book will expose you to universal truths that will change you forever. Find a comfortable and quiet place to sit as you open to the first page because you will not want to stop reading as Garnet unleashes revelation after revelation that will touch, move, and affect you in ways you cannot imagine, but will undoubtedly help you to (1) expedite your spiritual growth, (2) raise your vibrations, and (3) set things right on our beloved planet Earth for the human race and all other life forms who call this planet home. In these pages, you will find important universal words of wisdom and universal truths imparted by Garnet's guide, Albert, and many others – including the Council of Wise Ones and beings incarnated on other planets and dimensions. Prepare to learn about the Galactic Council and how we came to be on Earth, and just how powerful our words and actions really are. This is a book that I will refer to and quote from again and again, and I will be gifting all my friends and family with a copy of this significant guide to the evolution of humankind."

Sherri Cortland, ND – author of *Windows of Opportunity, Raising our Vibrations for the New Age, Spiritual Toolbox,* and *Guide Group Fridays*

"Who are we? What is our purpose? What happens when we die? These are some of humankind's most important and enduring questions. *Dancing Forever with Spirit* brings a fresh and exciting perspective to these ancient questions. Garnet Schulhauser shares the wisdom and insightful revelations learned from his spirit guide. It opens a window to the spirit world, sharing love, laughter and compassion, and not taking life too seriously. His account will bring comfort and insight to many during the most important times of our lives. This book is well written and enthusiastically recommended."

Mel Fabregas – host of *Veritas Radio*

"Garnet Schulhauser is back with his second book, *Dancing Forever with Spirit*, that takes readers on an incredible journey of enlightenment with Albert, his Spirit Guide from *Dancing on a Stamp*. In this journey, Garnet is shown the ins and outs of the Spirit World to understand our Earth, as well as other planets in the solar system and how these all interact with one another. You'll be amazed at the intriguing insights that Garnet shares with you! A definite page turner."

Jackie Wiersma, author of *The Zodiac Recipe: A Guide to Understanding You and Your Relationships*

"*Dancing Forever with Spirit* is a beautiful continuation of Garnet Shulhauser's first book, *Dancing on a Stamp*. Through interaction and astral adventures, Garnet and his spirit guide, Albert, offer the reader much needed information on a multitude of fascinating topics. As an Intuitive Medium, I recognize the significance and important of this book with its valuable and meaningful insight, which provides each one of us the opportunity to heighten our own awareness."

Shelly Wilson, Intuitive Medium and author of *28 Days to a New YOU, Connect to the YOU Within*, and *Journey into Consciousness* www.shellyrwilson.com

Dedication

To Kymera

Acknowledgments

I would like to acknowledge the many people who provided me with encouragement, inspiration, and support in connection with the writing and publishing of *Dancing Forever with Spirit*.

First, a hearty thank you to Dolores Cannon, who motivated me to get going on the manuscript, and to Julia, Nancy, Shonda, and Holly at Ozark Mountain Publishing, Inc. for their helpful support along the way.

I am grateful for all the encouragement I received from friends, family, and readers of *Dancing on a Stamp*, who urged me to continue my dialogue with Albert and write a sequel. There are too many of you to mention, but you know who you are.

Many thanks to Blake, Lauren, Colin, and Bergis for their unwavering support of my writing endeavors and to Cathy for her patience, understanding, and companionship during the many long days spent writing and rewriting the manuscript.

And a special acknowledgment to my granddaughter Kymera, whose arrival in August of 2013 inspired me to strive to make our world a better place to live for all future generations.

Table of Contents

Introduction

Since *Dancing on a Stamp* was released in October of 2012, my life has been a whirlwind of challenging and rewarding events. The release of my first book marked the beginning of a whole new chapter in my life—a time when I came out of the spiritual closet to announce to family and friends that I was a spiritual person who had been in regular contact with one of my spirit guides.

As my friend Sherri Cortland noted, my decision to come out of the spiritual closet was not an easy one to make. Even while I was conversing with my spirit guide and writing the manuscript for *Dancing on a Stamp*, I still struggled with the idea of actually publishing my book. I knew it would shock many of my friends and former colleagues because what I wrote was totally out of character for me—based on what they knew about me to that point. For over thirty years I had been a straight-laced corporate lawyer, and no one would have suspected my intimate connection with Spirit.

Right up to the time I signed the publishing contract with Ozark Mountain Publishing, I thought about shelving the whole project and sticking my manuscript in a drawer somewhere, unseen by anyone. But deep down inside I felt that publishing my book was the right thing to do even though it would cause large ripples in my world, and I would be shunned by some of my mates. In the end, I knew that if I did not publish my book I would regret it for the rest of my life. So I decided to take the plunge and let the chips fall where they may.

Overall, the good things have outweighed the bad. Although I lost contact with a few people, the vast majority of my friends stuck with me, and they applauded me for sharing my spiritual experiences. And most important, I have met many enlightened new friends who will continue to enrich my life in the years to come. *Dancing on a Stamp* has opened many new doors on my spiritual journey, and I have learned much from the experience. If I had it to do all over again, I wouldn't change a thing.

Dancing on a Stamp is based on the conversations I had with a homeless man named Albert who stepped out of the shadows one day to confront me on the street. Albert was actually one of my spirit guides in disguise, and he proceeded to answer all the eternal questions about life, death, and God, that I had been asking myself for many years.

Albert answered all of these questions, and many more, by revealing startling new insights about our true nature as eternal souls and the reason we incarnated on Earth. I wrote *Dancing on a Stamp* at his request so these revelations would be available to everyone.

My second book, *Dancing Forever with Spirit*, describes my latest adventures with Albert as he takes me on an astral journey to the Spirit Side and the Akashic Records, to other planets in the galaxy, and to the New Earth in a higher dimension. With Albert as my tour guide, I was able to view our planet and its inhabitants from a new prospective that gave me a much deeper understanding of where we fit into the grand scheme of the universe.

Albert showed me many examples of the abuse our civilization inflicts on our fellow humans, the creatures that share our planet, and Mother Earth herself, while providing sage guidance on how we can overcome these challenges by discarding our negative emotions and embracing love and compassion. Albert revealed that humans are fast approaching a crucial time in their development, and we must learn to expand our consciousness and reject the dark side before we self-destruct like some of Earth's civilizations in the past. And before we can hope to help other humans make the shift, we must first get our own houses in order by learning to quiet our minds and live in the present moment, which will help us hear the messages we all get from Spirit.

Albert's wit and wisdom during our astral excursions provided refreshing new insights into the cycle of life on Earth and the evolution of our souls. I hope you will enjoy reading *Dancing Forever with Spirit* as much as I enjoyed my adventures with Albert.

—Garnet Schulhauser

Chapter 1

The Adventure Begins

It was another Monday morning on this school called Earth. I slowly swung my legs off the bed, shuffled into the bathroom, and once again stared at my face in the mirror. I was not in a happy state of mind, and the mug staring back at me reflected my mood. It was not because I had to put on my navy pin-striped suit to go to work at my law firm. Thankfully, those days were long past, as I had retired from that career several years ago. I was frustrated because I had not been able to make contact with Albert for a couple of weeks, and it was not like Albert to shun me; he had always been there for me when I needed him.

And I really needed Albert right now. I had just begun to write the manuscript for my second book, a sequel to *Dancing on a Stamp*, and I needed some new revelations from Albert. Without Albert's wisdom I would be stuck in neutral, going nowhere. I was eager to write about all the new insights I hoped to glean from Albert, but I was beginning to fear the worst—that Albert had abandoned me.

For those readers who are not familiar with *Dancing on a Stamp*, it is a book based on a series of conversations I had with a homeless man named Albert who jumped out of the shadows to confront me one day when I was still practicing law. Albert had looked like a typical homeless man, with long, stringy hair, scraggly beard, and dirty, slept-in clothes. But instead of making a quick sidestep around him, I stood there like a deer caught in the headlights—transfixed by his brilliant, sparkling blue eyes that shone like two little blue stars. His gaze penetrated deeply into my very being, right down to the depths of my soul, and I sensed that he knew all the intimate details of my life—my fears and anxieties, my hopes and aspirations, and my deepest and darkest secrets. Despite feeling somewhat naked and exposed, I did not feel violated because at the same time his amazing eyes sent forth a gush of warm, unconditional love that permeated my whole body with an unforgettable sense of peace and security. I could have stood there forever, basking in his love. Ultimately, however, he broke my reverie when he said "why are you here?" before promptly disappearing.

When I found Albert on the same street the next day, he told me he was there to answer my questions and help me on my journey. Initially I was skeptical as he looked like he had slept in his clothes for weeks, and he smelled like a dead fish. But my intuition urged me to take a chance with this man—to see if he could really answer all the "big questions" in life I had been asking myself for years: *Who am I? Why am I here? What am I supposed to accomplish in my life? And what will happen to me after I die?* So I sat down on the bench that day with this homeless man, and our conversation began. I was surprised when Albert told me he was actually one of my spirit guides in disguise, and I was the only one who could see him as the homeless man. In fact, after our third meeting, Albert no longer appeared in the flesh and he spoke to me telepathically as a voice in my head.

Albert answered all my questions with wisdom, compassion, and humor, without preaching or lecturing. His responses felt right and rang true in my heart, and I knew what he told me was the "real" truth. And he shocked me one day when he asked me to write a book about our conversations so all humans would have access to his revelations. Although I was reluctant at first because I had never before written a book or even contemplated doing so, I soon learned it was futile to argue with Spirit. So I wrote *Dancing on a Stamp* with guidance from Albert, a wise spirit who proved to be amiable and unassuming.

Albert's revelations were often startling and always illuminating. Much of what he told me flew in the face of almost everything Christian holy men had been preaching for centuries and contradicted many of the beliefs I had been taught as a child, growing up in a very religious Roman Catholic family. It soon became clear to me, however, that his truths were preferable to most of the dogmas of the Catholic Church.

Albert revealed that we are all eternal souls who will live forever. We came from the Spirit Side before we were born, and we will return there after our physical bodies die. We were created by the Source (also called the Creator or God), exist as part of the Source, and we are connected to one another and to everything else in the Universe. We are beings of energy that spun out from the Source like sparks of light from the Central Sun.

We incarnated as humans by our own choice—no one made us come here. We came to this planet, which exists on a plane of dense matter, to learn and experience things that do not exist on the Spirit Side so we can grow and evolve as souls. Before we were born, we each prepared a Life Plan that set out the significant details and events of our proposed lives on Earth, including our names and places of birth, and the identities of our parents, siblings, spouses, children, and friends. We designed our Life Plans with a view to experiencing the events and learning the lessons we needed for our evolution. But our Life Plans (which we are not allowed to remember while on Earth) do not dictate everything that happens to us, because we have free will to act and make decisions during our time on this planet.

Contrary to what many organized religions believe, the Source does not control the events in our lives and it does not make rules for us to follow. There is no absolute right or wrong on Earth, and nothing we do will offend or disappoint the Source because the Source does not have any expectations for us. The Source wants to experience the Universe it created in all of its different facets by experiencing everything we encounter in our many different incarnations.

It follows that the Source will not judge or punish us for anything we did during our lives. All souls return to the Spirit Side after their physical bodies die regardless of what they did on Earth. This means murderers and terrorists return to the Spirit Side just like all the good people. And we can continue to incarnate on Earth over and over until we are satisfied that we have evolved to the extent necessary to graduate from this planet.

Albert described the Spirit Side as a wonderful place full of love, peace, and happiness, without any pain, suffering, or negative emotions. It is like the heaven described by most religions, a blissful and happy place full of interesting challenges in the joyful pursuit of wisdom. When souls return to the Spirit Side they can choose to return to Earth in another incarnation, remain on the Spirit Side as long as they desire, or incarnate into one of the millions and millions of other life forms in the Universe. Our souls are on a never-ending trek of exploration and evolution, an ebullient journey with no finish line.

Overall, I found Albert's revelations to be comforting and inspiring, and I was grateful he had asked me to recount them in *Dancing on a Stamp*. But my job as Albert's messenger was not finished, since he had divulged early on that I must write at least three more books after my first, and he would connect with me when the time was right to provide new insights for my next book. I had groaned a little when I heard this, although I knew resistance was futile. Even though I relished the prospect of more conversations with Albert, the thought of writing more books was somewhat daunting. At the time, I had wondered if there was a way I could wiggle out of this work program— maybe by feigning illness or senility; however, my intuition told me I could not fool Albert, so I took a few deep breaths and began my second manuscript. *Let the adventure begin*, I thought, hoping Albert would show up soon.

I tried everything that had worked in the past to connect with Albert. I sat on my chair in a quiet room and meditated for several minutes before silently reaching out to Albert in my usual fashion, but all I got back was the sound of my own breathing and the taste of my mounting frustration. So I called his name out loud several times— with no response except for the high-pitched barking from my little dog.

Finally, I resorted to desperation tactics, thinking that maybe Albert wanted to test my ingenuity. So I Googled "wise spirit Albert," and all I got were websites with Albert Einstein and Albert Schweitzer quotes. A search under "Spirit Side" was no better—the first listing was for *The West Side Spirit*, a Manhattan newspaper, followed by Sylvia

Browne's website, neither of which made any mention of Albert. I could almost picture Albert chuckling at my foolishness.

Then it happened. I was sound asleep in bed one night when I was startled by a strange noise coming from the doorway of my bedroom. I sat up and looked around, but I could not see anything unusual. My wife, Cathy, was sound asleep next to me, as was our little dog, Abby. Then I noticed a shimmering outline of a person standing in the doorway. This ethereal figure began moving toward me, and, when it reached the foot of my bed, I could make out its features. It was Albert in his homeless man disguise—exactly as he looked when I first met him on the street years ago.

"Where have you been, Albert? I have been trying to contact you for the past few weeks," I challenged him silently in my mind.

"I have been here, watching you," he responded as a voice in my head. "I wanted to be sure you were really primed for your next adventure. You must come with me on a trip, and when you return you will write about what you saw."

I was surprised to see Albert once again as the homeless man, although I could not fathom his reason for doing so. I was truly puzzled about the trip he mentioned because it was the middle of the night, and I couldn't get up and leave without telling Cathy where I was going and when I would return.

"What kind of trip do you mean? Where are we going and how long will I be gone?" I ventured.

"I will take you to explore your planet, other parts of the Universe, and the Spirit Side, so you will better understand what the Source has created and how you and the rest of humanity fit into the whole picture. You will travel with me in spirit form and leave your physical body behind. You will be back in your body before morning, and your wife will not be aware you were gone," Albert reassured me.

He held out his hand, which I grasped firmly as I rose from the bed. I turned to look behind—and saw my body still lying in bed, sound asleep. I realized then that I was now in astral form, as Albert and I slowly floated upward through the ceiling and into the night sky. I felt light and airy, like fine white gossamer floating in the breeze. I could see our house down below and the lights of the city, which appeared smaller and smaller as we ascended toward the stars.

We continued to rise until Earth looked like a small blue orb floating in the darkness of space. Then Albert motioned for me to turn around, and I could see a doorway in front of us. The door frame was lit up with bright, shimmering light, but I could not see anything past the doorway—only a velvety blackness without any stars. Albert led me through the doorway to an amazing scene on the other side that was beautiful and breathtaking. I stood there motionless as I tried to take it all in.

I was in a gorgeous meadow filled with lush green grass and dazzling flowers with hundreds of different iridescent hues. Majestic redwood trees guarded the far edges of the meadow. The cloudless sky was a brilliant blue, and everything was bathed in warm sunlight. I could not see the sun anywhere in the sky; it seemed like the sunlight emanated from everywhere.

Albert beckoned me to follow him, and we walked slowly up a gentle slope. The verdant grass felt like velvet on my bare feet. My head was filled with a delightful, almost intoxicating, perfume that wafted up from the flowers, and my body glowed from the warm light that enveloped me like a diaphanous sheath. *What a wonderful place to take a stroll*, I thought, somewhat whimsically.

When we reached the crest of the hill I could see a group of people on the other side, gathered near the bottom. Behind them in the distance I could see a city with white buildings and spires that shimmered in the light. As we got closer to this group I could make out several of the faces, and my heart skipped a beat. I recognized my mother and father, my brother Brian, my grandmother Hartney (who was the only grandparent I knew on Earth), and all of my aunts and uncles who had passed away previously. From behind the group a small black puppy sprang toward me, his little tail wagging his whole body. It was Oscar, our miniature Schnauzer who had passed on several years before. I knelt down to greet Oscar as he jumped up to lick my face. I gave him a warm hug and told him it was great to see him again. Everyone in this group had warm radiant smiles that lit up their faces as they approached me, one by one, to give me a loving embrace. I felt like I had arrived home after being away on a long journey. No words were spoken—it wasn't necessary—as the feeling of unconditional love that enveloped me spoke volumes.

They all appeared to be healthy and happy, like they were when in the prime of their lives on Earth. Although they did not look like how I last remembered them on Earth, I had no trouble recognizing them, except for a few of them who stood off to the side waiting for an introduction. I soon learned they were my grandparents, uncles, and aunts who had passed away on Earth before I was born.

Then my mother stepped forward, and I sensed she needed to tell me something. Even though Mom was still smiling warmly, I was a little apprehensive. While on Earth, Mom had been a very religious person—a devoted Roman Catholic all of her life. She had faithfully followed all the rules of the Church and firmly believed that worshiping God in the ways prescribed by the Church was the only sure way to reach Heaven. And she had been determined to make sure her husband and five children would all join her in Heaven, even if she had to drag us kicking and screaming.

I was concerned because I had not been kind to the Catholic Church in *Dancing on a Stamp*, often poking fun at their arbitrary and illogical rules and beliefs. And since many of Albert's revelations contradicted the teachings of the Church, I wondered now if my mother was upset with me for writing my book.

Mom gave me another warm hug and allayed my fears: "Welcome home, Garnet. I know what you are thinking, but there is no need to be concerned. If I were still on Earth, I would not be happy about what your book said about the Church. But now that I have passed over to the Spirit Side, I can see the big picture. I agree with everything you wrote in your book, and I think you did a great job in conveying Albert's messages to humanity.

"As you can see for yourself, everyone in your family who has already crossed over from the Earth plane has made the transition to the Spirit Side, safe and sound. The Spirit Side is truly a wonderful place full of love and joy, without any of the negatives found on Earth. You are only here for a short visit because you must return to Earth to complete your unfinished business. You have more books to write so other people can hear Albert's truths. Wherever you go, do your best to encourage everyone to treat all humans, all creatures, and Mother Earth herself, with the dignity and respect that flows from living a life of love, forgiveness, and compassion. And be sure to comfort those who are grieving the loss of a loved one by reassuring them that all souls return Home after their human bodies die regardless of what they did or did not do while on Earth. The passing of a person on Earth should be a time for celebration, without any tears, as everyone will eventually be reunited once again on the Spirit Side."

I breathed a sigh of relief and responded: "That's great, Mom. Somehow I knew you would not be upset—but it's wonderful to have the confirmation. Last year when I was speaking to a book club group, someone asked me what my mother would think about my book. I responded that she would not have liked it if she were still on Earth, but I ventured that you would have a much different view now that you were back on the Spirit Side. After the meeting was over, a young lady approached to tell me she was a medium, and when I was answering the question about your view of my book she could see you standing behind me, giving me two thumbs up."

"That was me, all right. I have been watching over you the whole time since I returned Home, even though you may not have been aware of my presence. Now it is time for you to continue your journey with Albert. We will see each other again before too long. Farewell for now."

Albert had been standing quietly off to the side, watching and waiting, but now he motioned it was time to move on. I waved farewell to my relatives and followed Albert on a path through the meadow toward the gleaming white city ahead of us. As we got closer, its buildings, topped with domes or spires, loomed larger and more awe inspiring with each step. Finally we reached the edge of the city and stood before an entry portal, with spectacular white pillars topped by a gleaming arch.

"What is this place?" I asked Albert.

"This is one of our cities on the Spirit Side, known as Aglaia. Come with me, and I will show you around," Albert replied.

As we entered through the portal I was taken aback by the amazing vista in front of me. The streets were paved with smooth gray stones that looked and felt like slate. The white walls of the buildings shimmered in the light and felt smooth and warm to my touch, reminding me of polished marble.

The streets were filled with people, all with beaming, smiling faces that projected a sense of peace and joy. They all seemed to be going somewhere, except they walked with the leisurely pace of pedestrians who were in no hurry to get to their destination. The clothing they wore was stunning, with a plethora of vivid colors in many different designs and styles. I felt like I had been plunked down in the middle of a glamorous costume ball. Some of the garments I recognized from history books; they looked like the clothes worn by people on Earth from many different countries and eras. I noticed saris from India, togas from Ancient Rome, kimonos from Japan, doublets from medieval England, and flapper dresses popular during the Roaring Twenties. Many of the outfits were unfamiliar to me, but resplendent nonetheless.

While I stood there, transfixed and totally in awe of the indescribable beauty that paraded before my eyes, Albert explained that souls on the Spirit Side do not have a specific gender, and they can choose to appear as either male or female based on the sex they identified with most often during their incarnations on Earth. Souls are free to change their gender at any time, or they can discard their Earthly appearance and manifest themselves as globes of light. They will often dress in the clothes they enjoyed wearing in one of their previous lives on Earth, and they can change their attire as often as they wish. Every soul is easily recognizable to others by its inherent energy pattern, regardless of its external appearance. He pointed out that the clothing that was unfamiliar to me was worn in some of the ancient civilizations on Earth that left no historical records.

Once again, Albert gave me a gentle nudge as he led me down the broad bustling street. After a few blocks, we entered an open square with a fountain in the center, spewing forth a stream of sparkling water that cascaded back into the reflecting pond below. The plaza was filled with people strolling casually or sitting at tables. Off to the far right I could see a choral group standing on a low stage. They wore flowing scarlet robes adorned with silver sashes, and the carol they sang was the most beautiful music I had ever heard—like a chorus of angels singing a song of joy. Their singing was so enchanting that Albert had to tug at my arm several times to break the spell.

Albert guided me toward a tall stately building at the far end of the plaza, a magnificent structure with Grecian pillars lining the front. When we reached the front of the building, which he called the Hall of Wisdom, we entered through the wide-open doorway. At the end of a long hallway we stopped in front of a grand door made of shining burnished brass, and Albert gently announced our presence with the round door knocker. Upon hearing the word "enter" from inside, Albert opened the door and we stepped into the room.

It was large and circular, with a high domed ceiling. The room was well lit without any visible light fixtures, as the light seemed to emanate from the walls. In the center of the room was a table in the form of a semicircle, with the open section facing the door. The table was black and smooth, like gleaming granite, and it seemed to float in place without any legs or any other visible means of support.

There were eleven people seated at this table, facing the center of the semicircle where Albert and I stood. They wore long gold-colored robes with a white sash tied around the waist. They looked very regal, with snow-white hair and smooth unwrinkled skin. Seated at the center was a striking woman with intense blue eyes. I sensed this person was the chair of the panel.

"Welcome, Garnet. We have been expecting you. And thank you, Albert, for arranging this meeting," the chairperson began with a warm smile. "We asked Albert to bring you here so we could give you our message to humanity for inclusion in your next book. We would like you to disseminate our entreaties to all the people on Earth."

"Who are you, and what is this place?" I responded.

"This is the Spirit Side, the place you came from before you incarnated on Earth. It exists at a much higher vibration frequency than Earth, and it can't normally be seen by people on Earth. It exists beyond the veil and is known to some people as Home, the Other Side, or Heaven. You will return here once again when your life on Earth is finished, but your visit this time will be short because you still have many things to accomplish before you cross over.

"My name is Sophia, and this is the Council of Wise Ones. It is our job to oversee Earth and the souls who incarnate on your planet. We provide guidance and counseling to all souls before they begin their lives on Earth, and we assist returning souls with the analysis of the lives they have just completed. Our main function is to help souls design Life Plans that will enable them to grow and evolve through their experiences on Earth. We try to ensure that the lives that are chosen are not too difficult for a particular soul (which can hinder its evolution if it rebels too much against the harshness of the life) or too easy, without appropriate lessons to be learned and challenges to overcome. We are here as well to counsel souls currently incarnated on Earth—to assist them with any adjustments to their Life Plans that may be desirable. Like all other souls, you travel to the Spirit Side every night during sleep to consult with this Council and your guides, but you don't remember these trips since you pass through the shroud of forgetfulness every morning when you return to your body.

"You will remember this visit because we want you to write about your experiences on the Spirit Side and your other adventures with Albert. We want you to tell everyone what you will see and learn on this journey. We think humans are ready for these new insights, which we hope will help them make the transition to a new awareness.

"Are you willing to undertake this task?"

"Albert has already twisted my arm about writing a second book, so it's a moot point at this stage. What would you like to tell me?" I ventured.

"To begin, we want you to understand the transition that is now happening on Earth and its implications for your fellow humans." With a small wave of her hand, a large holographic sphere, filled with swirling blue and white vapors, dropped down from the ceiling and hovered above the floor. The swirling vapors quickly dissipated, leaving behind a crystal clear image of Earth, as seen from space. I could see the outlines of North and South America and Western Europe, which were partially covered with white clouds. It was breathtaking to see Earth from this viewpoint.

Sophia let me stare at Earth for a few minutes, and then began: "Your planet and its human inhabitants are at a major inflection point in their history. Humans are in the process of expanding their consciousness and transitioning to a higher vibration frequency, but they still need a lot of help to achieve this. If this does not occur in a timely fashion, the consequences could be tragic for Earth and all of its inhabitants.

"This shift will allow those who have increased their vibratory rates to transition to Earth in a higher dimension—a place often referred to as the New Earth—where the negative aspects of life on Earth don't exist. The New Earth is a place where all of its creatures, including humans, live in peace and harmony, without conflicts or wars and without killing and maiming—a planet filled with love, compassion, and forgiveness. In the New Earth humans do not pollute the atmosphere, the water, or the soil, and they do not abuse the other creatures on the planet. And all the negative emotions that have been prevalent throughout human history, like fear, anger, hate, jealousy, and greed, are nonexistent.

"Some humans have already made the transition and many others are in the process of making the shift. Unfortunately, there are millions of humans who are not even aware of what is going on around them.

"Human civilization is at a very advanced stage right now. You have created advanced technology that has made life much easier for most people; however, this technology has not been universally beneficial to everyone. Many people on Earth do not have enough food to eat or clean water to drink, and not everyone lives in a comfortable house, has access to the Internet, or lives free from the fear of arbitrary violence. Furthermore, your advanced technology, with its weapons of mass destruction, is capable of destroying all living creatures on your planet if it is used for the wrong purpose.

"Earth has been home to many advanced civilizations in the past, like Lemuria and Atlantis, and none of them has survived. Several were destroyed by the actions of some of their citizens, driven by greed and the lust for power, who used technology to pursue their own goals. And whenever these civilizations collapsed, humanity had to start all over again. Humans are now once again at a similar stage of development, and they are facing the same crucial test: can they avoid destroying their civilization so all humans will have the opportunity to transition up the vibratory ladder, or will they crash and burn like these other civilizations that flopped in the past.

"Mother Earth herself is becoming impatient with humans and their abusive behavior. She is weary of humans who abuse other creatures and pollute her oceans and rivers, her fertile soil, and her atmosphere, with toxic chemicals, noxious emissions, and tons and tons of unsightly garbage. And make no mistake that Mother Earth is capable of fighting back—she can increase the number and intensity of your natural disasters, such as earthquakes, floods, hurricanes, tornados, and volcanic eruptions, as a way of hitting back at humans. Ultimately, as a last resort, she has the ability to wipe out human civilization so that she can start over again with a clean slate.

"For humans to avoid destroying their civilization with their own technology, or being wiped out by natural disasters, they must hasten the transition to the New Earth by increasing their vibratory rates and making the ascension to a new level of consciousness. To do so, they must learn to control their negative emotions and embrace love, compassion, and forgiveness.

"That is why humans must be especially vigilant during these times. Those people who are enlightened must be diligent with their efforts to help all humans make the shift, so that human civilization will continue to flourish in the New Earth."

I stood there silently, soaking it all in. This was a lot to comprehend all at once, but I sensed the urgency in Sophia's voice. "What can I do to help the cause? What can one person do to alter the mindset of millions of people?"

"You must do your best to make all people aware of the situation and encourage everyone to work hard at making the transition by writing about your visit here and the other things you will encounter on your journey with Albert. You see, this is just the first stop on your adventure—Albert will take you on trips to explore your planet and other parts of the Universe, and you must describe it all in your book.

"This Council has been helping your cause in many different ways. We have been increasing the pace of the messages we are sending to humans about the coming transition, because time is becoming crucial. Our messages are sent through a number of different channels and messengers, with the hope that more and more people will understand the problem and become part of the solution. Increasingly, we have enlisted more advanced souls to incarnate on your planet to assist humans through their leadership and wisdom. And many advanced civilizations on other planets in the Universe have answered our call for help, and their assistance has been very positive. Albert will introduce you to some of these extraterrestrial life forms (ETs) on one of your trips so you can see for yourself.

"This is enough for now. You must continue your journey of exploration with Albert."

Sophia and the other members of the Council rose from their chairs and filed out of the room. Albert and I left the Council chamber and relaxed on a bench in the plaza outside.

As I sat there enjoying another magical song from the choral group, I tried to digest what Sophia had revealed to me. Much has been written lately in spiritual and metaphysical books about the New Earth and how humans must increase their vibrations so they can rise up and join the New Earth, leaving the Old Earth behind, as part of the transition from the third dimension to the fifth dimension. I was curious as to what Albert thought about these theories, in light of what Sophia had told us.

"First of all," Albert began, "the use of the words 'New' and 'Old' are monikers that make sense only on Earth with its perception of time as a linear progression from past to present to future. As I mentioned to you before, this concept of time is only an illusion because linear time does not exist on the Spirit Side. In reality, there is no past or future, only the present.

"The New Earth is not a future event. The planet Earth exists simultaneously in several different dimensions, each with different vibratory rates. The Old Earth, which is the Earth that you know, is on the lowest step of the ladder—the dimension with the lowest vibratory rate and densest matter. The New Earth is further up the ladder in a dimension with a higher vibratory rate. But the New Earth is not something that will happen in the future—it has always existed simultaneously with the Old Earth.

"Humans living on the Old Earth have vibration rates that match the vibration frequencies of their planet. If they want to transition to the New Earth they must increase their vibratory rates to match it. Some humans have already done this, and many more are working toward this goal. Not everyone living today on the Old Earth, however, will make the transition in their current lifetimes, but their souls will return to the Spirit Side when their physical bodies die because no one is ever left behind. Once they are back on the Spirit Side, they can decide if they want to reincarnate into a human on the Old Earth to help the remaining humans make the shift, or they can choose to incarnate into a human who has already made the transition to the New Earth."

"Is the New Earth the same as the Spirit Side?" I wondered.

"No, it is not the same. The New Earth still exists on the physical plane, only it is not as dense as the Old Earth because of its higher vibratory rate. Humans on the New Earth still have physical bodies, although they have shed all of their negative emotions and live in a world of love, peace, and harmony. And because they have learned how to focus their thoughts into powerful streams of energy, they are able to easily manipulate matter and manifest whatever they desire. So there are no shortages of material goods on the New Earth and no need for humans to fight one another for the things they all want. As a result, negative emotions like jealousy, greed, anger, and hate do not exist.

"Humans in the New Earth often live for several hundred years, since they can control the aging process, resist disease, and heal bodily injuries. Their physical bodies die when their souls decide it is time to return to the Spirit Side, not as a result of old age or disease.

"Souls on the Spirit Side do not have physical bodies; they are like beings of pure energy. So while the New Earth has some of the positive characteristics of the Spirit Side, it is not the same. The New Earth is partway up the vibratory ladder, while the Spirit Side is at the very top."

"What will become of the Old Earth when all humans have made the transition?" I wondered.

"The Old Earth will continue to exist simultaneously with the New Earth. When all humans have made the shift, it will go through a natural cleansing process to rid itself of all the garbage and pollution left behind by humans. Once this has been completed, it will be ready once again to accept new life forms to nurture and grow. These new life forms will be seeded by the ETs under the direction of the Council, and a new cycle will begin."

"What happens if the remaining humans do not make the transition because they have destroyed all life on the Old Earth with their pollution or weapons of mass destruction?" I wondered.

"In that case, the souls of those killed in the destruction will return to the Spirit Side, except they will not have the option of incarnating again on the Old Earth. If this happens, Old Earth will have to go through a much longer cleansing process before it is ready for new life forms. In the worst-case scenario, it will remain as a barren and lifeless planet with no further prospects for harboring life."

While I pondered that very unsettling thought, Albert led me out of Aglaia and through the doorway leading out of the Spirit Side. As I floated down to Earth and back into my bedroom, I told Albert I was eager to continue my adventures with him so I could find a way to help my fellow humans make the transition before it was too late.

I was grateful I had a chance to visit with my relatives on the Spirit Side, and especially happy my mother had given me the thumbs up on *Dancing on a Stamp*. Although Albert had told me all souls return to the Spirit Side when their human bodies die, it was a pleasant bonus for this to be confirmed to me during my trip to Aglaia.

The next morning I woke up back in my body with the memories of my trip still crystal clear in my mind. I went for my usual morning walk with Abby, enjoying the fresh ocean air and the fragrant perfume of the rhododendron blooms. I admired the majestic Douglas fir and Western red cedar trees that lined the road, the neatly trimmed juniper hedges between the houses, and the dazzling hydrangeas, begonias, and peonies in the flowerbeds. I could see the Gulf Islands dotting the Strait of Georgia and the lofty coastal mountains of the mainland in the background. I smiled at the music of the songbirds and laughed at two hummingbirds chasing each other around the red and yellow feeder hanging from our eaves. *It would be a pity if this beauty and splendor might disappear forever*, I thought, as I yearned for another visit from Albert so I could learn what I needed to do to help save my planet.

I didn't have to wait very long this time, as two nights later Albert appeared once again in my bedroom and beckoned me to follow. My astral body easily slipped out of my physical body like before, and we rose up and up into the darkness of space. I had no idea where we were going this time, but I sensed that Albert had a few surprises up his sleeve.

Chapter 2

Proteus

I glided effortlessly behind Albert until we reached a point high above Earth, which hung in the blackness of space like a jeweled pendant. I was mesmerized by the grandeur of my home planet, but I knew Albert had not brought me here just to see the sights.

"Where are you taking me this time?" I pumped Albert.

"We are going to visit a watery planet many light years from Earth so you can meet a few of its inhabitants," Albert explained.

"So how will we get there?"

"I have arranged for a dog sled to pick us up. It won't go very fast, but it has a monitor for in-flight movies. I am thinking you will have time to watch a few thousand movies during the trip, so I hope you don't mind reruns or subtitles. And, as an added bonus, you can curl up with the dogs if you get cold."

"Very funny, Albert. I can see your humor hasn't improved much since our first meeting. You need to hang around comedians on the Spirit Side so some of their humor will rub off on you."

Albert grinned mischievously and shrugged his shoulders. Then he grasped my arm, gave me a reassuring wink, and pointed toward Orion. Earth and all the stars suddenly disappeared, leaving nothing but the blackness space. After a few seconds, the stars reappeared, and I noticed we were hovering in space above a brilliant blue planet that reminded me of Earth. Its surface was covered with an azure ocean without any landmasses, with wispy white clouds gathered near the equator. Behind me I noticed a bright sun that was similar in size and appearance to our own Sol. As we dropped down toward the surface, I could clearly see the calm waters that sparkled in the sunlight, looking much like the oceans on Earth. We continued to drop until we submerged into the crystal-clear water.

Beneath the surface I saw an underwater world very much like the subterranean landscape of the Caribbean Sea that I remembered from several past snorkeling adventures. It was teeming with brightly colored fish, long black eels, and many larger fish that looked like sharks. The seabed was partially covered with coral and a profusion of aquatic plants basking in the warm light from the sun.

I floated languidly in this undersea world, enjoying the splendor around me without the need to surface for air. Then I felt a gentle tug from Albert as he motioned for me to follow him.

"Where are we, Albert?" I said as we glided through the water.

"We are on the planet Proteus, which orbits a sun in your galaxy a few hundred light years from Earth. This entire planet is covered with the ocean, and there are no landmasses above the water. All life on Proteus is aquatic, and most of its species are similar to those found on Earth."

"Why did you bring me here?"

"I want you to meet someone. Follow me," as he floated toward a large structure resting on the seabed. As we got closer, I could see that it was similar to the coral reefs on Earth, except much larger. Near the base I spotted two familiar-looking creatures—the larger one looked like a humpback whale while the smaller creature reminded me of a dolphin.

We were greeted by a soft, melodious voice emanating from the dolphin look-alike.

"Welcome to Proteus. My name is Aldine and this is Horace. We are delighted to meet you, and we are grateful to Albert for bringing you here."

"You two look like the dolphins and humpback whales we have on Earth," I noted.

"We are the same life forms as your dolphins and humpback whales because Proteus is where the dolphins and humpback whales on Earth originated. Many eons ago, when Earth was very young, the Galactic Council determined that Earth's oceans were ready to support life forms, so they seeded your planet with sea life and aquatic plants from our planet. That is why everything around you looks so familiar," Horace chimed in.

"How did these life forms travel to Earth?" I asked.

"The Galactic Council arranged for the beings from the planet Nibiru to transport our flora and fauna to Earth in their faster-than-light spacecraft. In fact, all sea life found on Earth today originally came from Proteus," Horace continued.

"Who is the Galactic Council?" I wondered.

"The Galactic Council is the body of wise beings that oversees our galaxy. One of their functions is to seed life throughout the galaxy on planets that can sustain it. Once they have chosen a planet for new life, they seed it with life forms from planets with similar conditions, which is why they matched Earth with our planet," Aldine responded.

"So why did you want to meet with me?"

"We asked Albert to bring you here so we could give you a message to pass on to all humans on your planet," Aldine explained. "First, you should know that we continue to communicate telepathically with our brethren on Earth, even though we are hundreds of light years apart. Although we do not have technology as humans know it, we are much further advanced than humans in many respects. We have learned how to control our emotions so that we don't abuse one another or any other creatures on our planet. Negative emotions, like fear, anger, and hate, do not exist on our planet. We live in peace and harmony with each other and with our planet. We learned long ago that love will always trump fear, and compassion and empathy will allay the need to judge others.

"And because we have conquered our negative emotions, we were able to increase our vibratory rates and expand our consciousness to the point where we can communicate with our brothers and sisters over vast distances. Although our water-covered planet does not have humans, we know all about humans on Earth—and we don't like what we hear.

"We want humans to know it is wrong and abusive to hunt, trap, and kill our kin on your planet, as you have been doing for many years. We have been listening to the cries of anguish from whales that have been harpooned by ruthless humans and from dolphins that are hunted for food or imprisoned in your water parks and aquariums. And despite their frequent attempts to communicate with humans to get them to stop the carnage, their efforts have been futile. Humans, despite their large brains and advanced technology, do not hear these cries for help. Most humans have not been able to raise their consciousness to a level high enough to hear our pleas, mainly because they are too wrapped up with greed and arrogance.

"Humans need to realize that all life forms in the Universe form part of the Source. We are not separate entities, but part of the whole. So you should not think of dolphins, whales, and other sea life as merely unthinking, unfeeling animals to be used (or abused) as humans see fit. We are sentient beings who have been reaching out to your race for centuries, except all we get in return, for the most part, are violence and disdain. We acknowledge that there are many humans who oppose this brutality and who do their best to stop the abuse, but these people do not control your planet. Even though considerable progress has been made in the past few decades to curtail the exploitation of our kin, like the moratorium on commercial whaling, much more needs to be done.

"And to add to the perils our Earth cousins face every day, humans have endangered all sea life on your planet by dumping untreated sewage, toxic chemicals, and other waste products into your oceans, lakes, and rivers.

"We do not understand the unbridled arrogance of the human race. They act like Earth was put there for their own exclusive use and the other creatures that share your planet do not matter. Earth and all of its other creatures do not deserve such abuse; however, we seem to be powerless to stop this from happening. To be honest, your planet would be much better off without any humans. We do not have humans on Proteus, and we enjoy a healthy, balanced ecosystem without any pollution.

"When we pleaded with the Galactic Council for help, they told us they could not directly interfere with the activities of humans on

Earth, but they could help us persuade humans to change their ways. This is why you are here. We ask you to return to your planet and spread our message to the multitudes. We implore you to accept our plea to help our family on Earth."

I was stunned and dismayed by what I heard. I could actually feel the hurt and anguish flowing from Aldine as she spoke. I knew this was a cry for help that I must answer.

"I accept your request," I responded. "I will take your message back to Earth, and I will do my best to ensure it is heard by all humans."

I gave them both a hug and nodded to Albert that we should be on our way. Albert took my hand, and we rose up through the water and up into the brilliant blue sky of Proteus. When this beautiful planet was nothing more than a small blue orb, Albert pointed his finger at the stars, and we once again entered the total blackness of space. Seconds later, we emerged back in our solar system and continued down toward Earth. We floated through the clouds, down through the roof of my house, and settled gently into my bedroom. My wife and little dog were still sleeping peacefully beside my body.

I woke at the usual time the next morning, back in my body. At first I thought maybe I had experienced a vivid dream, except the details were so crystal clear that I was absolutely positive my trip with Albert was for real. I felt a strong urge to sit at my computer to record everything that happened before the details slipped from my memory.

When I opened the e-mail inbox on my computer and saw all the spam waiting for me, I wondered if we wouldn't be better off living with no technology like the whales and dolphins on Proteus. It seemed that whenever a new invention was developed to make life easier and more productive for all of us, certain malefactors always found ways to exploit the new technology for their own selfish purposes, to the annoyance and detriment of everyone else.

All I had to do was respond to the spam and I could get diet pills to lose fifteen pounds in ten days, purchase a guaranteed risk-free investment that would return 30 percent profit in two months, learn the secret to increase my libido, and buy a magic lotion that would grow new hair in a matter of days. Then I realized my secret was out in the open: Someone had found out I was actually fat, stupid, sexually challenged, and bald.

But I was on a mission, and the spam would have to wait. After our visit to Proteus, Albert told me he would be back in a couple of days to show me some very troubling events happening right now in our planet. I was not keen to see what he had in store for me, but I knew it was futile to argue with him. So I braced myself for his next visit.

Chapter 3

What on Earth Are We Doing?

Albert was true to his word. On the next night following my visit to Proteus, I woke from a deep sleep to find Albert standing in the doorway of my bedroom, gesturing for me to follow him. I rose smoothly from my bed, leaving my body behind, and followed Albert as we floated up and up into the night sky until Earth was a small blue orb floating in the darkness of space.

"Where are we going this time?" I asked.

"We are going back to Earth so you can see some of the abuse humans are dishing out to animals on your planet," he responded.

With that, Albert began his descent toward Earth, and I followed him effortlessly. We drifted down through the clouds and emerged over the Pacific Ocean near Indonesia, heading toward a fishing boat with a flurry of activity on its deck. The crew was busy reeling in their longlines, baited with dolphin meat, which had hooked dozens and dozens of hammerhead, thresher, and tiger sharks. While the sharks were still alive, men with sharp knives cut off their fins and threw the bleeding sharks overboard, where they would die slowly from asphyxiation or be eaten by predators. Albert explained that the fins were harvested to make shark fin soup, which was a delicacy in Chinese cuisine. As the fins were more valuable than shark meat, the rest of the shark was discarded to make more room for the fins. Although shark finning has been banned in a number of countries, the practice continues in many parts of the world, to the extent that several species of sharks are on the brink of extinction.

I watched with disgust at the slaughter of the sharks until I could no longer stomach this brutality. I turned my back on the fishing boat and signaled to Albert that I had to leave. Albert whisked me away from the bloodbath on the boat, and we rose up through the clouds, reemerging moments later above the African continent. We dropped down into a secluded part of Zimbabwe to witness another scene of carnage—a field strewn with the bodies of several dozen dead elephants. A group of poachers was busy sawing off the ivory tusks with chain saws and tossing the plunder into the back of their trucks. The valuable ivory would be sold on the black market to customers in Asia who would use it for elaborate carvings and traditional elixirs. I was deeply saddened by the sight of these magnificent creatures lying lifeless on the plain, and I shuddered to think that this slaughter would continue unless drastic action was taken.

"Killing elephants for their ivory has been going on for centuries," Albert advised, "And recently poachers have become more sophisticated. Instead of shooting the elephants with rifles they are now killing them with poison, which is quicker and easier. The elephants you see here died from ingesting cyanide planted by these poachers.

"This is another example of the abuse that goes on every day on your planet, not just with sharks and elephants, but with many other species that are hunted and killed by humans for their horns and other exotic animal parts to satisfy customers who do not know, or do not care, how they were obtained. And none of this killing is essential for the survival of any human. I could show you dozens more examples, but I think you get the picture.

"Your people have to realize that the other creatures on your planet were not put there to be abused by humans. Homo sapiens must rid themselves of their intolerable arrogance when it comes to other animals. All creatures on Earth have an equal right to live their lives as it was intended, and humans do not have a special status in animal kingdom—they just think they do. The abuse of other animals will continue until enough enlightened humans demand a stop to these practices. Although a lot of progress has been made in recent years, you still have a long way to go."

"This leads me to an obvious question, Albert. Should humans refrain entirely from eating meat and seafood? Should we all become vegetarians?"

Albert looked at me intently with his penetrating blue eyes and responded: "Even though your question is very complex, I will try to answer it in a way you can understand. First of all, there are no absolute right or wrong actions on Earth, in that the Source does not make rules for humans to follow. But we all have rules and guidelines for our conduct on Earth that we set for ourselves as evolving souls.

"It is the goal of every soul to grow and evolve by experiencing life on Earth and learning the lessons we set for ourselves. Every soul that incarnates on Earth has a strong desire to prod their physical bodies to discard all negative emotions and embrace only love and compassion for everyone and everything.

"In this context, it is wrong to kill animals for sport or to harvest exotic body parts that are not essential for survival. You should not step on a bug on the sidewalk because you do not intend to eat it, and it is not causing you any harm. It is very callous for humans to think it is all right to kill animals for the thrill of the hunt. When it comes to killing animals for food, however, the answer is more complicated.

"In the animal kingdom, it is not wrong for a lion to kill and eat a gazelle or for a fox to eat a rabbit, as this is something they must do in order to survive. They do not kill for sport; they kill what they need to feed themselves and their cubs, and they do not feel any hatred or anger toward their prey. Likewise, it is not wrong for a bison to trample a wolf that was about to kill her calf, or for a human mother to swat a wasp that was going to sting her infant.

"With humans, it is not so clear cut when it comes to killing other animals for food. Historically, humans have been omnivores because they ate animal flesh as well as vegetation. In the early days, humans did not have the food choices available today, so they had to survive by eating the flesh of any animal they caught and by scrounging for edible fruits, berries, and roots.

"Many vegetarians on your planet argue that eating animal flesh is wrong because it is unnatural for humans. They believe humans are actually herbivores from a physiological perspective, and they rely on esoteric anatomical arguments to support their view. They cite things like the length of humans' intestinal tract in relation to their body length, the relative size of their mouths, and their tendency to chew their food extensively, as proof that humans are more like herbivores than carnivores.

"It is pointless, however, to argue humans are supposed to be herbivores because some of their physical characteristics are similar to herbivores, when historically it is clear humans have been practicing omnivores for over two million years. And since the Source did not have any specific intentions for humans when it created them (just like it did not make any rules for humans to follow), it should be apparent that it is not unnatural for humans to eat animal protein since that has been their practice for as long as your records have been kept.

"But this does not mean humans should necessarily continue to be omnivores. In the beginning, humans had limited choices for food, and they had to function as 'opportunivors' by eating whatever happened to be available at the time. In recent years, most people in the developed world have an extensive array of fruits, nuts, berries, grains, and vegetables available at the local supermarket and, armed with modern scientific knowledge about what is essential for a nutritious diet, they can live healthy lives without consuming animal flesh. Although vegetarianism has been around since the days of ancient Greece and India, its popularity has increased significantly during the last fifty years.

"Vegetarians adhere to their practice for several reasons. Many believe eating animal flesh is detrimental to their health and physical well-being. Others feel it is morally wrong to kill other animals for food. And some vegetarians believe raising animals for food is harmful to the environment and an inefficient way to feed the people on Earth. More recently, some people have become vegetarians because they believe the consumption of animal protein is a deterrent to raising their vibratory rates and expanding their consciousness.

"Now that so many humans have the ability to eat healthy and nutritious food without consuming animal flesh, does this mean that killing animals for food is wrong? Provided the animals are killed in a humane way, and their bodies are consumed for food, the decision should be left up to each person on an individual basis. After thousands of years as omnivores, it would be unrealistic to think that humans would change this practice overnight. As humans continue to evolve and increase their vibratory rates, more and more humans will intuitively cut back on the amount of animal flesh they consume until it is eliminated completely from their diets. This will be a gradual process that should not be forced on people.

"Not only will there be a slow and steady shift away from animal protein, but humans will begin to cut back on solid food of any kind, eventually consuming only liquids containing all the nutrients needed for a healthy body. Ultimately, at some point in the future, humans have the potential to progress to a state where they won't even need to consume liquid food; they will be sustained by directly tapping into the energy of the Universe. In the meantime, people should consider their options and do what feels right to them. The transition will happen smoothly as humans raise their vibrations, but the pace of change will be different for every person."

This was a lot to absorb in one day, so I asked Albert to take me back home where I could digest everything I had seen on this eye-opening trip. But Albert demurred: "I know you are dismayed by what you saw today, but before you return to the comfort and security of your home I want to give you more food for thought by showing you some of the damage inflicted on your planet by thoughtless and uncaring humans."

So we sped away from the elephant slaughter and emerged from the clouds above a factory town in southern China. As we got closer, I could see the black smoke spewing forth from the forest of industrial chimneys. When we entered the black smog above the factories I could barely see the ground below. Although I could not smell or breathe the air in my astral form, I had no doubt I would have been choking if I had been there in my physical body.

"What a horrible blot on Earth's atmosphere," I lamented to Albert. "How can any living creature breathe this stuff without eventually dying a horrible death?"

"This is another form of abuse fostered by humans," Albert responded. "Emissions like this all over the world are poisoning

Earth's atmosphere and causing major problems for Mother Earth and all of her inhabitants. And this is only one example of human-generated pollution. Humans are poisoning rivers, lakes, and oceans with garbage, toxic chemicals, and other human waste at an alarming rate. They have been contaminating your farmland with herbicides and pesticides for decades and are chopping down acres and acres of oxygen-generating trees every day in the rain forests of your planet. Most of this activity is supposedly for the betterment of human civilization, although the side effects of these activities are delivering the opposite result.

"Mother Earth is like a living organism that has been abused by humans for their own pleasure for centuries. If humans do not cut back and eliminate their pollution, they will have to suffer the consequences. As Sophia warned when we met with the Council of Wise Ones, Mother Earth has the ability to fight back, and she had already started her counterattack by dishing out more severe natural disasters around the world, which will continue to escalate until the pollution has stopped or she has managed to rid herself of the cause. Humans should not underestimate the determination of Mother Earth to fix the problem."

"You make a chilling point," I ventured. "What can I do to turn things around?"

"Every single person can help the cause, and many people acting in concert will make a huge difference. You must spread the word as much as possible and ask everyone you touch to do the same. Eventually, the governments on Earth will hear the message and they will be forced to make changes or face the wrath of their citizens. Although a lot of progress has been made in the last fifty years, humans still have a long way to go in the quest to minimize pollution."

Albert's warning sent a shiver done my spine, but I could tell he wasn't finished yet. So I girded my loins for his next blast. As usual, Albert did not disappoint as he continued his rant.

"One of the quirks of Homo sapiens as a species is that they not only abuse their planet and the other creatures that live on it, they also abuse other humans through violence and neglect. Human civilization at this point has the capability to ensure that all people can enjoy the basic necessities of life wherever they may live, except this has not happened because the wealthy nations do not share enough with the poor countries, and the rulers of the poor nations often squander their country's resources on themselves or on armaments. These imbalances in the ownership and distribution of resources on your planet continue to be a blot on humanity because too many of the privileged people do not care enough about the 'have-nots' to instigate change.

"Let me show you what I mean. I will take you to a couple of other places in present-day Earth so you can see for yourself."

Our first stop was in New York City at a posh restaurant in midtown Manhattan. We slipped through the walls and entered a private dining room filled with a couple dozen men and women dressed in expensive business attire. Albert explained that this party was to celebrate the completion of the merger of two public companies. The people in the room were executives of the merged companies, investment bankers who provided advice on the merger, and lawyers from the two large law firms that handled the legal aspects of the transaction.

They were all enjoying cocktails, and the chatter was animated and jovial. Then the waiters wheeled in a cart loaded with French champagne (at a cost of $300 a bottle) that was served to all the guests. After several toasts to honor the completion on the merger and the hard work of all those involved, they sat down at the tables so dinner could be served. Albert told me it was a set menu of five courses (foie gras, lobster bisque, beef tenderloin, crème brûlée, and assorted cheeses and fresh fruit) at a cost of $225 per person, served with bottomless bottles of white and red wine costing $100–$150 per bottle. To finish off, the guests were served fine cognac, vintage port, and twenty-five-year-old single malt scotch, along with Cohiba cigars.

At this point, a couple of the younger guests, who had consumed a few too many glasses of wine, decided to liven up the party. They each grabbed a bottle of champagne from the cart, shook them up, and began spraying each other with the foaming liquid. It looked like a scene from the dressing room of the Super Bowl champions. Everyone in the room laughed at these antics, and no one seemed to care that this expensive champagne was being wasted.

"This is an example of how some privileged humans treat themselves to extravagant displays of crass consumption," Albert advised. "Now come with me to see someone living in the other extreme."

Albert led me out of the restaurant and we glided smoothly across the Atlantic until we were over Somalia, in the Horn of Africa. We floated down into a small village and entered a tiny hut. Inside was a young emancipated woman in her late twenties who was nothing more than skin and bones. She was sobbing uncontrollably while clutching the limp body of her dead child, who looked to be around three years old.

Albert explained that this woman had lost her husband several weeks before when he was shot by militants. She had little money and no other family members to help her, and she had struggled to provide food and water for herself and her child. Several days before, her child became very ill with dysentery from drinking contaminated water, and, because there were no doctors or medical facilities anywhere close to her village, the young mother had to watch her child slowly wither away and die.

My heart went out to this young mother, and I wished I could have given her some comfort. But as I was there in astral form, she could not see or hear me, and I could not touch her. It was heartbreaking for me, and I felt helpless.

"Do you see the contrast between this scene and the one in New York?" Albert chimed in. "One of the major problems with humanity is that many humans live in comfortable homes, enjoy plenty of good food and drink, and have access to state-of-the-art medical facilities, while millions of other people do not have enough food to eat or clean water to drink. This is even more shameful when you consider the wasteful extravagance of some of the privileged people. This imbalance in the distribution of resources on your planet is one of the things impeding humanity's advance toward greater consciousness and higher vibratory rates.

"The people at the party in New York did not directly cause this woman's anguish in Somalia, but they also did not do anything to help the cause. Imagine the difference if they had canceled their party and donated the money instead to a charity that provided aid to the poor people of Somalia. None of them would have suffered without the party, and their donation would have alleviated much suffering in Africa.

"I could show you plenty more examples of affluent countries squandering resources while homeless people live in the streets, seniors struggle to buy food, and many families subsist in poverty. Not to mention all the humans in the destitute countries who die each year from malnutrition and disease.

"And then you must consider all the direct premeditated injuries and deaths humans inflict on one another every day. If you listen to your news programs it will not be difficult to find examples of this abuse: homicides, terrorist killings, civil wars, religious conflicts, and genocide, just to mention a few. It seems that whenever some progressive nations take a step forward, other nations take a step back. In the developed world, it is the right of every child to receive an education funded by the state, while in other nations girls, for religious reasons, are not allowed to go to school. And what would you say to a child in your country who asked you how it was possible that a young girl was shot by grown men merely because she had campaigned for the right of girls to be educated the same as the boys? Indeed, humans, how is it possible that these things still happen on your planet?"

I had no answer for Albert, and I was no doubt red-faced with shame over the conduct of my fellow humans.

"This is all very depressing, Albert. Is there any hope that the Homo sapiens on this planet can turn things around, or are we doomed to fail yet again?"

"Of course there is hope for humans, which is why I took you on this tour. Later, I will show you the good news. To paraphrase one of your famous sages, Yogi Berra, it ain't over till it's over. Even though humans have made a lot of 'wrong mistakes' to this point, they can still pull the fat out of the fire by focusing on what is important and by understanding that winning is 80 percent mental concentration, while the other half is physical. And most important of all, the next time you come to a crucial fork in the road, you've got to take it."

"How can you joke at a time like this?

"Because it is much better to laugh than to cry in your beer. If you can't laugh at your foibles and the predicament humanity is in, you will never get out of this mess. Let me take you back home so you have time to digest what you saw today. Then I will return to show you some things you never contemplated in your wildest dreams."

Chapter 4

Learning from the Past

A few days went by with no sign of Albert, so I was ready for him when he finally reappeared in my bedroom. We followed our usual routine and floated up to our rendezvous point high above Earth. Then I followed Albert through the doorway to the Spirit Side, past the beautiful meadow, and into Aglaia through its stately portal. Albert led me down a wide street that opened off the main square, and we stopped in front of a tall rectangular building with wide stone steps leading up to a gleaming bronze door. Albert explained that this was the Hall of Records, which contained the Akashic Records.

We marched up the steps, through the massive doorway, and stood at the edge of a large foyer with a high ceiling that emanated light from an elegant crystal chandelier. Three wide hallways branched out from the foyer like spokes of a wheel, each lined with doors on both sides. We sauntered down the corridor on our left and entered one of the unoccupied viewing rooms, which was empty except for a large holographic globe filled with blue and white swirls.

"Why did you bring me here?" I ventured.

"As you know, the Akashic Records contain the complete details of every life that has ever been lived anywhere in the Universe. I want to show you how Life Reviews work, which are an essential part of the transition back to the Spirit Side after souls finish their lives on Earth. Every returning soul comes here for its Life Review, where it can review and analyze everything that occurred in its last life. In your Life Review you will be able to observe your past life like you are watching a 3-D movie, with the ability to view it in slow motion and pause the action from time to time in order to get a better perspective. You will be able to review your life in chronological order or in any other sequence that makes sense to you. And you will also be able to 'relive' all or parts of your life as though you were back in your human body.

"One of the more beneficial aspects of your Life Review is that you will also be able to hear the thoughts and feel the emotions of all the people you interacted with while on Earth. So if you had said some cruel words to a coworker one day, you will be able to feel this person's hurt and rejection in response to your belligerence. Or if you had brought flowers to your elderly aunt in the hospital, you would sense the deep gratitude she felt for your thoughtfulness. This feature of your review will give you a better understanding of how your words and actions affected other people.

"You should understand, however, that Life Reviews are not intended to make you feel guilty or remorseful. Their purpose is merely educational—to give you a better perspective on your life so you will get the most from your experiences. The goal is to help you recognize the mistakes you made and the lessons you failed to learn, which will be very useful to you when planning your next life.

"When you are reviewing your life, you will have the benefit of knowing what you intended in your Life Plan, and this will help you understand where you strayed off course as a result of the messages you missed from your spirit guides. Your guides will be there to help you analyze the effects of your wrong turns, missed opportunities, and failed lessons, except no one will judge you or give you a grade for the life you just completed; it will be up to you to evaluate your performance based on the criteria you set for yourself before you were born.

"When your review is finished, you will plan your next incarnation. You can spend as much time as you like resting and recovering from your recent life, especially if you had a hard life or you suffered a violent death. There are no timetables on the Spirit Side, and no one tells you what to do or when to do it. And you will be able to access the vast body of knowledge available on the Spirit Side to help you plan your next move, including the Akashic Records that will allow you to review all of your previous lives on Earth. The Wise Ones and other souls in your soul group will always be available to answer your questions and offer advice."

"Seems like a well thought-out process," I offered. "Why did you bring me here now, since I have not yet finished by current incarnation?"

"I think it would be good for you to experience a short preview of what your Life Review will be like after you cross over. On our last excursion I showed you examples of how humans have abused other humans, the other creatures on your planet, and Mother Earth herself. Now I want you to understand that sometimes your words or actions can be hurtful without any deliberate intention on your part. I have chosen certain segments of your life to demonstrate the importance of always putting yourself in the place of others before you speak or act so that you will treat them with kindness and compassion instead of abuse."

Albert waved his hand over the holographic sphere and the wispy swirls gave way to a crystal-clear image from my past—a scene from my classroom when I was in the seventh grade. I could see myself sitting at my desk listening to my science teacher and twirling a pencil between my fingers. I scanned the room and remembered all the faces and names of my classmates, even though I had not seen any of them for quite some time. Then the bell rang to signify recess, and we all piled out of the room and raced outside into the sunny schoolyard.

Most of the boys headed toward the soccer field to play a short pick-up game. As I began a slow lope to keep up with the other guys, I heard a plea to "wait up" from behind. It was my chubby friend Adam who was struggling to keep up.

"Hurry up, fatso," I shouted jokingly. "We don't have all day."

Suddenly, the scene in the sphere shifted to focus on Adam's red puffy face. I could hear his thoughts as if they were spoken out loud:

Hey, guy, I know I'm fat—but it's not my fault—I get it from my dad. I am trying my best to keep up with you, but you can run too fast. You have no reason to make fun of me. You hurt my feelings and embarrassed me in front of the whole class, and I thought you were my friend. I wish I could disappear down a gopher hole, never to be seen again.

I could feel his emotions swirling around his head. It was a mixture of embarrassment, rejection, and hopelessness. The pain Adam felt recoiled through me like a wave of nausea, and I felt sick to my stomach.

And then it was over, and the sphere returned to its pattern of swirls. I looked at Albert in dismay.

"I had no idea my off-the-cuff remark to Adam had such a devastating effect on him. I did not intend to offend him. I was merely poking fun at his roly-poly body," I lamely explained to Albert.

"Such is the case all too often with you and most other humans. You tend to speak without thinking about how your words might affect others. Even innocuous 'jokes' can cause others much embarrassment and discomfort. In the example you just saw, Adam was very sensitive about his weight and the fact that he was not good at sports. He felt betrayed by someone he thought of as a friend. He never forgot that incident, and he blanched every time after that when he heard the word 'fatso,' even if it wasn't aimed at him."

"I feel terrible. I wish I could somehow make amends."

"What happened that day long ago is history," Albert advised. "It is water under the bridge, and you cannot change it. And since Adam died of a heart attack in the late 1990s, you won't be able to make things right with him when you get back to Earth. The only thing you can do is give him a big hug when you cross over to the Spirit Side one day yourself."

This incident with Adam reminded me about the problems we seem to have these days with bullying. In the last few years, I have noticed a number of news stories about teenagers committing suicide because of bullying. Often it results from cyber bullying—where a child is tormented on various social media sites. Sometimes it is the old-fashioned kind of bullying through verbal and physical abuse at school. It is very sad to hear about these cases, and it makes me wonder what motivates children to torment others to this extent.

Bullying has been around for centuries, well before the Internet and social media sites. But now cyber bullying has added a whole new dimension to this shameful and hurtful practice; it makes it convenient for the bullies to be abusive without being in close physical proximity to their victim. This allows the taunting to become somewhat depersonalized and easier for the perpetrators to pull off from the comfort of their own homes.

Although bullying can occur in any age group, it seems to be most prevalent among teenagers. This is likely because adults have matured enough to understand the harm it can cause, coupled with the fact that the target will be better able to stand up to the bully and fight back. Peer acceptance is very important to a teenager and the lack thereof can sometimes be overwhelming, often to the point of suicidal thoughts. And very often the parents of the victim are not aware of what is happening because their child is reluctant to bring them into the loop, or they don't take steps to help their teenager because they don't appreciate the severity of the problem.

When I was a teenager, I witnessed physical bullying at school— typically a bigger boy picking on a smaller one. Often there was verbal bullying by excessive teasing and name-calling. And sometimes the bullying was in the form of a child being excluded from a circle of friends and shunned, most often with teenage girls. But I could never understand the motivation for bullying. Was it because the perpetrators were really mean-spirited people who intended to be cruel, or was it a case of the bullies not fully appreciating the effect of their actions on their victims.

When I raised the issue with Albert, he weighed in with this wise observation: "Bullying has been an age-old problem with humans on your planet. It can be in the form of children bullying other children, or adults bullying other adults at work, or even one nation bullying another nation. Its root cause usually stems from fear or anger, and it often has a negative spin-off—since someone who is bullied will be inclined to bully another person as a way to get even and vent their frustrations.

"The reason bullying is more prevalent among teenagers is that they have developed beyond the innocent years of childhood when they are beginning to think like adults but don't yet have the wisdom and maturity to handle their daily interactions in a thoughtful way. Teenagers also receive messages from their souls and spirit guides, although they often do not recognize and accept this guidance, and they let their negative emotions rule their lives. They do not have a fully developed empathy for other people, and thus they seldom stop to consider how their words and actions may affect other teenagers.

"And like younger children, teens will copy what they see in adults. If parents often react to people and events in a negative fashion, their teens may emulate these responses when they interact with other teens. And this is especially so if parents are in the habit of bullying their own children.

"The best way to stop bullying begins at home. Parents should strive to avoid negative responses to events and demonstrate to their children that it is important to show love, compassion, and forgiveness to all other people. Children should be taught at an early age that all humans have souls and that all souls are connected to the Source and to one another. They should be encouraged to listen for messages from their guides and not allow their negative emotions to rule the day.

"It has been a long uphill battle for humans to stamp out bullying, and now the problem has increased to a large extent with the advent of social media. The good news, however, is that governments and schools in several of the developed countries have recognized the problem and are actively looking for ways to combat bullying. Every step in the right direction should be supported and applauded by all humans."

I silently wished all the bullies in the world, and their parents, could have heard Albert. Except I knew this was not going to happen, so I sat back in my chair and waited for Albert's next move.

"Let me show you another example of how you hurt someone you cared for because you were too wrapped up in your own little world," Albert continued. I winced as Albert waved his hand over the sphere and the blue and white swirls disappeared, giving way to another scene from my past.

I recognized it to be Calgary, the city where I worked as a lawyer for most of my life. And then I spotted something very familiar—it was the house we lived in before I retired from the law firm. The picture focused on our family room, which was exactly how I remembered it during the many years we lived in that house. I judged by the light that it was late afternoon, and no one was around except for our little dog

Oscar (a miniature Schnauzer), who was sleeping in his bed by the sliding glass doors that led to our back yard.

"Why are you showing me this?" I said to Albert.

"I want to show you that all animals on Earth have feelings and emotions, just like whales. To give to a better perspective on what happened this day, I am going to let you hear and feel Oscar's thoughts and feelings."

Then I heard the familiar noise of the garage door opening, and I could hear Oscar's thoughts as he eagerly trotted to the hallway leading to the garage.

That must be the alpha man, he thought. *He has been gone all day, and I can hardly wait to see him.*

Oscar's little stub tail wagged furiously as he waited in the hallway. Then the door swung open and I entered from the garage, wearing a navy pinstriped suit and looking tired after a long day at work.

Hey, my friend, I am so happy to see you. How about a few pats?

I hung my topcoat in the closet and walked right past Oscar without acknowledging him in any way. I could feel the hurt and anguish Oscar felt as I passed him without so much as a simple hello.

Oh no! What have I done now? I have been waiting all day for you to return and now you ignore me. Did I do something wrong? Did I offend you somehow? Whatever I did, I promise not to do it again. Please, please come back and gently stroke my head so I will know you still love me. You are the most important person in my life—and I need to feel your love.

If dogs could cry, the tears would have been rolling down Oscar's little cheeks. Instead, he slunk slowly back to his bed and rested his head on his crossed paws, totally dejected.

I was saddened and embarrassed by my hurtful disregard of Oscar. I did not recall that particular incident, but I must have had a bad day at the office. Nonetheless, that was no excuse for the way I ignored my little dog. He did not deserve to be treated that way.

I glanced at Albert and tried to convey my dismay: "I feel awful about what I did to Oscar that day. I had no idea dogs could feel rejection and sadness, or that a simple greeting meant so much to Oscar. I wish I had it to do over again."

"I didn't show you this to make you feel bad. I wanted you to understand that animals are actually more intelligent than you think. They have emotions and feelings not unlike humans, and they deserve to be treated with respect. Like you heard on Proteus, humans are extremely arrogant and self-centered, and a lot of people believe animals were put on your planet for the pleasure of humans. And all too many humans think that killing and abusing other creatures is acceptable because they are just dumb animals who do not really matter.

"Humans need to understand that animals also have souls that will return to the Spirit Side when their physical bodies die. They are having a journey on Earth to learn and experience things, just like you. In fact, you have had several animal incarnations before you began your human lives, which is not unusual for souls who come to Earth. You do not remember any of these lives while you are here, but you will remember them all once you get back to the Spirit Side."

"This was not an easy scene for me to relive, Albert. But now I have a better understanding of animal life on this planet, and I will look at things differently from this point forward."

"Let me cheer you up," Albert offered. "You have made numerous mistakes so far in your life, but you did some really good deeds as well, even if you don't remember any of them."

With another wave of his hand the holographic sphere now displayed a scene from my days as a lawyer. I could see myself sitting in my office reading e-mails on my computer. Then there was a gentle knock at the door and a young associate lawyer, Trevor, cautiously entered and sat down in one of the chairs facing my desk. His face was ashen, and his eyes were wide with fear. When I asked if I could help him, he blurted out that he had messed up. He explained that he had failed to file a document with the Stock Exchange before the deadline, which could delay the completion of our client's financing. He apologized profusely and then sat quietly, with a look of dread on his face.

I was upset about the missed deadline, but it was not the end of the world. Mistakes do happen, and I remembered I had made my fair share of them already in my career.

I sat quietly for a few seconds before speaking. "Not to worry. Everyone makes mistakes from time to time. We can fix this up with the Exchange tomorrow and hopefully this will not impact our client adversely. You should learn from this mistake so you can move forward from here. Go home and get some rest, and we can meet bright and early tomorrow morning to call the Exchange."

The scene in the sphere shifted to focus on Trevor's face, and I could hear his thoughts and feel his emotions: *Whew! What a relief. Oh thank you, God, for helping me out. I was worried sick about this. And thank you, Garnet, for being so understanding. I will never make this mistake again, and I will always remember this day if I ever have occasion to deal with a similar situation when I am a partner.*

I did recall that day as I watched the replay, although I had no idea Trevor was so distraught over his mistake. I thanked my lucky stars I had handled the situation the way I did. No one deserves to feel so bad over a simple mistake. After all, making mistakes is to be expected since no one is perfect. The crucial test we all face is how we react to our mistakes and the mistakes made by others.

I was relieved when Albert motioned for us to leave the room so I would not have to face any more distressing scenes from my past. He told me it was not his intention to bludgeon me with mistakes from my past; he only wanted to demonstrate how easy it was for humans to say and do things every day without considering their effect on others.

We left the Hall of Records, floated down to Earth, and back into my bedroom. I waved good-bye to Albert before I slipped back into my sleeping body. The next morning I walked outside, looked up toward the sky, and silently mouthed an apology: *Sorry, Adam and Oscar, for all the hurt I caused you. Please forgive me.* I sensed they were both listening to my invocation with smiles on their faces, and I knew we were all good.

After the preview of my Life Review things were never quite the same. The intensity of the feelings I had felt from Adam, Oscar, and Trevor still burned in my memory. I vowed to think before I opened my mouth and consider what emotions my words might stir up in other people. I truly wanted to avoid causing embarrassment or hurt feelings to others, and I was pleased my Life Review preview was having a positive effect on my interactions with other people.

Even little Abby noticed a change in my demeanor as I strived to be more patient with her when she stopped to sniff every pole and fire hydrant on our daily walks and when she barked to go outside for the umpteenth time after I had settled comfortably into my recliner chair.

There was one drawback to engaging my mind for too long before I put my mouth into action; I was concerned I might appear to be slow or dim-witted to other people, which was especially hard for someone who had always prided himself as a man skilled at quick wit and fast verbal retort. In the end, I took comfort from something Mark Twain said once when he noted that sometimes it is better to remain silent and be thought a fool than to open one's mouth and remove all doubt. Silence was definitely preferable to mindless babbling.

Life on Earth was clearly no walk in the park, as Albert liked to remind me whenever I whined about my lot in life. He kept telling me I was chosen to be one of his messengers to promulgate his revelations to the masses, although I don't remember applying for the job. But I couldn't stop now because Albert had aroused my curiosity after we left the Hall of Records. He had hinted he would be back soon to show me some things about human civilization on Earth that would shock me to the core, and I could hardly wait for his next visit.

Chapter 5

Win Some, Lose Some

When Albert reappeared in my doorway once again, with an extra sparkle in his eyes, I didn't know if I should run and hide or follow him like a little lost lamb. Albert settled the matter by grabbing my hand and yanking me out of my body, while flashing an impish grin.

As soon as we reached our usual rendezvous point high above Earth, Albert divulged his plan for this trip. "I have shown you some of the deliberate abuse that happens every day on your planet, and the unintentional harm that can result when people do not carefully consider the effects of their actions on other people and creatures. As you heard from the Council of Wise Ones, humans are now approaching an important crossroads, and they must decide which path to take. They can continue to harm one another, the other creatures on your planet, and Mother Earth herself, in which case they may suffer a tragic collapse like other civilizations in your past. Or they can choose to stop the carnage by discarding their negative emotions and expanding their consciousness, which will lead them to a wonderful existence in the New Earth.

"I am going to show two civilizations from Earth's past, one that made the transition and one that didn't. What would you like to see first: the good news or the bad news?"

"If you must show me more bad news, then let me have it first, Albert."

Albert nodded his head and continued: "In many cases, these societies had made great advances with technology, and their way of life was easy and free from material concerns. Their downfall was often caused by a certain segment of the populace, usually the leaders and scientists, who experimented with energies they did not fully understand and could not control. These people were driven by ego and the lust for power, which caused them to take unnecessary risks. When their experiments went awry, there would be major shifts in Earth's equilibrium, resulting in earthquakes and tsunamis. Quite often, entire landmasses sank into the ocean, killing most of the people and destroying all the advanced technology.

"There were always a few survivors who managed to escape the annihilation, and they were forced to start all over somewhere else without their technology or the knowledge to recreate it.

"Humans are aware of a few of these civilizations, although most mainstream historians still deny their existence. The two most famous ones are Atlantis and Lemuria. Someday in the not-too-distant future your archeologists will discover the remains of these civilizations on the ocean floor, and all doubts about their previous existence will be put to rest. For now, it is useful for humans to understand what led to their downfall so the pattern does not repeat.

"Humans have once again developed advanced technology that has been used, for the most part, to make life easier and more enjoyable. But there is the danger this technology could be misused to the detriment of all humans and creatures on your planet. Humans have the capability to destroy all life on Earth and render your planet a barren wasteland. This would be an unthinkable tragedy and something that must be avoided at all costs.

"Let me take you back to the Hall of Records so I can show you an advanced civilization from a long time ago that did not survive."

We glided into the same room in the Hall of Records, and Albert waved his hand over the holographic globe to conjure up a new scene. We were looking at Earth from above, as the scene in the globe morphed into a close-up view of an island with tropical vegetation sprawling over the landscape. The globe displayed the outlines of a city in the distance, with tall buildings that gleamed in the sunlight. As our view shifted into the city, I could see the streets filled with people dressed in garments that looked like togas from Ancient Rome. They looked much like humans today, except they were taller and slimmer.

They appeared to be happy and carefree, as most of them were smiling or chuckling as they engaged in animated conversation.

The buildings were constructed with highly polished beige stones that reflected the sunlight. The streets were paved with light green bricks that looked like the surface of a clay tennis court. The city was beautiful and serene as it exuded a sense of peace and security.

"This is the civilization that existed on an island in the South Atlantic Ocean known as Atzlan. The people who lived here were healthy and content because their advanced technology provided everyone with all of the essentials for a happy life. They were free to work on projects if they desired, or they could spend their time learning or enjoying recreational activities. They had developed advanced medical tools to heal injuries and prevent disease, which allowed them to live much longer than humans in your society.

"Their downfall resulted from their attempts to find a way to travel faster than light so they could explore the universe. Their scientists began to experiment with a warp drive that was designed to use antimatter to create a wormhole in the space-time continuum. Even though they had no real need to travel to other star systems, their eagerness to expand their empire beyond the solar system caused them to throw caution to the wind and experiment with energy they did not fully understand.

"Unfortunately, when they tried to open the space warp it triggered massive earthquakes and tidal waves and Atzlan sank to the bottom of the ocean, where the remnants of this civilization are now buried beneath the silt.

"All of their technology was destroyed, and the few survivors who had been exploring Central America at the time had to start over with Stone Age tools and know-how.

"I won't show you the day of destruction—you would find it too distressing. I brought you here to show you how great civilizations can be destroyed when they experiment with forces they cannot control."

"Now let me cheer you up and show you there is hope for your civilization to move up to a new dimension. Not all the advanced civilizations in Earth's past have been wiped out; some of them succeeded by increasing their vibratory rates and ascending to a higher dimension. These civilizations are still thriving today, and I will take you to visit one of them," Albert offered.

Albert explained that the Universe was composed of countless different dimensions that occupied the same space but existed at different vibration frequencies. This meant that the life forms living in one dimension would not normally be able to see or feel other life forms or objects in a different dimension.

Earth is on the lowest level of vibrations, with dense mass, which means everything moves very slowly compared to the higher dimensions. On Earth there is always a noticeable gap between a thought and its manifestation, which all souls find frustrating compared to life on the Spirit Side. (Albert explained that it was like standing in molasses up to your waist while trying to run a 100-meter sprint.) The slow-motion events on Earth give humans an opportunity to contemplate their actions as they wait for events to unfold. This is a learning tool for the souls incarnated on Earth—a way for them to better understand the consequences of their free-will actions.

I followed Albert out of the Hall of Records, and we exited the Spirit Side through the entrance portal. To the left of the Spirit Side doorway I noticed another portal, which Albert described as an interdimensional passageway. We floated through this opening into total darkness before emerging back into the starlight high above Earth, which Albert said was my planet in a different dimension with a higher vibratory rate. We drifted down toward the Americas and touched down somewhere in Central America.

We landed in a broad river valley, lush with green grass, colorful flowers, and majestic Sequoia trees. There was a village a short distance from us, hugging the banks of the broad, slow-moving river. The river water was crystal clear, and I could easily see the rocks and water plants on the bottom. We sauntered leisurely toward the village, enjoying the sweet smell of the flowers and warm sunlight on our faces.

What a perfect place for a picnic, I thought, as we entered the outskirts of the little town. The buildings were all one or two stories and painted in gentle hues of blue and green. The walls were constructed from a smooth, clay-like material, much like pottery. They had circular bases and domed roofs, with openings in the walls for windows and a door.

The people in the village looked like humans from my Earth, and they were all lean and fit and in robust health. They wore simple knee-length tunics in soft pastel colors with wooden sandals on their feet. There were children of all ages playing in the streets, and their infectious laughter resonated throughout the village. The adults, who all appeared to be in their twenties or early thirties, proudly displayed their golden tans on smooth, unblemished skin. Their smiling faces and easy laughter suggested a carefree and happy existence.

"This is Earth in your present time in a higher dimension, often referred to as the New Earth," Albert explained. "The people you see are descendants of a human civilization that existed long ago in your Earth's past in the area known to you as Central America. They were an advanced civilization, although they did not have advanced technology. In the early days of their civilization, they struggled with the difficulties typically encountered by other human civilizations. They incarnated as humans to experience life on Earth and to learn the lessons they needed for their evolution as souls. They were not allowed to see through the veil or remember where they came from, and they had free will like humans on your Earth.

"These conditions generated all the negative emotions that are prevalent in your society—like fear, anger, hate, and greed. They lived in a very hospitable climate with an abundance of nourishing vegetation readily available, which meant they did not have to fight one another for material goods and did not need to consume animal flesh to survive. Eventually, all this natural abundance, coupled with strong leadership from their spiritually aware citizens, reduced the conflicts in their society and allowed humans and animals to live in peaceful harmony.

"This transition to enlightenment was nurtured by a core group who learned to communicate with Spirit through meditation. They recognized that the negative emotions of their fellow citizens could be eliminated entirely if everyone understood who they were, where they came from, and their purpose for being on Earth. This inspirational group proceeded to teach all the others the benefits of living without negative emotions by embracing love and respect for all humans and creatures on the planet.

"Over time, their patient guidance and benevolence won the day, and this civilization entered a wonderful era of peace and harmony for all people in their society, along with respect for all other creatures and Mother Earth herself. And they did this without developing advanced technology, mainly because they had no need for it.

"But then dark clouds began to loom on the horizon; they discovered that another human civilization was encroaching on their territory. This other civilization was primitive and brutal because its people were still immersed in negative emotions, and there were many bitter conflicts within their society. They had developed crude but effective weapons that could kill people and destroy buildings, and they were inclined to use them frequently to gain material possessions or satisfy their lust for power.

"This encroachment was a great concern to the idyllic society, which had no desire or weapons to fight the barbarians. Nor did they have any means of transportation to flee the impending danger. So their spiritual leaders came up with a miraculous plan to save their civilization, a plan gleaned from their communication with Spirit. They concluded that their best escape route was through a mass ascension of all their people to a higher dimension where they would be free from the menace—a place where they could continue to live in peace.

"To accomplish the mass ascension to the new dimension all citizens would have to increase their vibratory rates to a much higher level, and they knew this could not happen if there were any negative emotions still lingering in the populace. Fortunately for them, these nasty emotions had been mostly eliminated long before, and all that was needed was a final purge of any that remained.

"With guidance from Spirit, they organized a gathering of all their people in a large field beside their village. The enlightened ones explained their plan to the assembly and led everyone on a deep meditation by repeating a special mantra. After an hour of intense concentration, one of the leaders rose and gave the command 'ascend,' whereupon their surroundings became blurred and obscured, like they were surrounded by a thick fog. Then they all stood up in unison, and the fog slowly dissipated. They found themselves standing in the same field beside their village that looked the same as before, except their lookouts reported that the approaching army of philistines was nowhere to be seen. They had achieved a mass ascension to a higher dimension—to a New Earth that was free of all negative emotions and free from all warlike humans.

"What you see in this village are the descendants of the people who made the ascension. In this higher dimension, the people do not suffer from injury or disease, and they have learned to arrest the aging process. Typically, they will abandon their bodies when their souls want to return to the Spirit Side."

We continued down the street until we came to the town square lined with tables and chairs, with a fountain in the center that spewed sparkling water high into the air. Several of the tables were filled with people engaged in animated conversation or merely sitting quietly and enjoying the sunshine. Most were sipping from clear glass goblets containing colorful liquids that looked like smoothies.

We strolled to a table occupied by a man and a woman who smiled warmly when we approached. They did not seem surprised by our appearance and motioned for us to sit down at their table.

"Good morning," Albert began. "I am Albert from beyond the veil. And this is my friend from Earth in a lower dimension. I brought him here so he could see a human civilization in a higher dimension."

"Welcome to our village," the female smiled. "My name is Zeranda, and this is my companion Eten. Would you like a tour of our village?"

"That would be great," Albert responded, as we rose up and followed the couple into the center of the plaza.

Zeranda began by waving her arm around the square. "This is our central gathering place, where we like to congregate for conversation and companionship. There are no bars or restaurants in this square or anywhere else in town, as we only consume liquid food developed from the many fruits and vegetables that grow naturally in our fields and forests. Our food is dispensed from taps located in every dwelling, freely available to everyone.

"As a result, we do not consume animal protein, and all creatures can live out their natural lives without interference from humans. Our food is perfectly nutritious and balanced and contains very effective prophylactics to ward off disease, along with medicinal cells that help to regenerate injured body parts. And because we have learned how to slow down the aging process, we can live for several hundred years.

"Everything we need for a healthy and happy existence—food, clothing, shelter, education, recreation, and entertainment—is provided free of charge by our Council of Citizens. We have no need for money, and we don't have any crime because there is no reason to steal or to harm another human. This gives us the freedom to pursue knowledge and happiness without having to worry about jobs or careers.

"Our people are not ruled by negative emotions, and we do not live in fear of not having enough or becoming sick or injured. And we do not fear death—since we know it is only a transition back to the Spirit Side.

"Without negative emotions, we are free to embrace love to the fullest. We treat all other humans and animals with dignity and respect. We do not pollute the land, the ocean, or the air, and we honor Mother Earth for all her gifts.

"We study your Earth and its history in our schools, and we know the conditions that exist for humans in your dimension. You are at a major transition point in your civilization—a time where more and more humans will be expanding their consciousness as they increase their vibratory rates. And what you see here is one example of what you will get after this shift. Welcome to the New Earth."

"This seems to be an idyllic existence," I ventured, "but wouldn't your lives be a little boring? You don't have jobs or careers, and you don't have to strive to overcome disease or injury to your bodies. So where are your challenges? What keeps you interested in life?"

"Our lives are actually very vibrant and fulfilling," Eten responded. "We are always in the pursuit of knowledge because there are so many things to discover in our vast Universe. Our challenge is to learn as much as we can about life wherever it may exist to help us choose our next incarnation after we return to the Spirit Side. Exploring other worlds and learning new things is very rewarding and it allows us to grow and evolve as souls."

"Do you get married and have children?" I wondered aloud.

"We don't have spouses or other exclusive attachments," Eten continued. "Our children are conceived in special incubators by joining sperm with eggs that have been extracted from volunteer donors. Since we aim to maintain a constant population level, we only replace those humans who have ended their incarnations. When the babies have completed their gestation, they are assigned to nurturing humans who provide them with loving care and attention in a healthy learning environment. They are raised in a collective society and do not have parents and siblings like families in your world. We prefer to operate like one large family where everyone loves and cares for everyone else on an equal basis. Our adults engage in sexual activities freely and openly, and there is never any jealousy or possessiveness."

"I think you have described your society very well, and I can hardly wait to make the transition myself," I responded. "I hope to see you again soon."

I gave them both a farewell hug before Albert and I rose up into the clouds and glided back through the dimensional doorway to hover once again above my Earth.

"So you see," Albert explained, "not all highly evolved human civilizations have ended in catastrophe. I took you to the New Earth so you can tell all other humans on your planet that there is hope for much better things to come. All you need do is focus on your goal and eventually you too will be able to live in peace and harmony. The transition is very achievable; it has been done before. But humans on your Earth must first rid themselves of all the negative things that hold them back, and they must do so before they lose control of their technology and destroy all life on their planet."

"I hear you, Albert, and I know what my marching orders are," I responded. "Take me back home so I can get to work."

"Before I leave, I have good news to share with you. Your civilization will not be left to flounder blindly on its own because you have friends in high places who have been discreetly helping humans make the shift—and they will continue to do so as long as it takes. On my next visit I will introduce you to some of them so you can see for yourself."

I nodded my agreement as Albert led me down toward Earth and back into my bedroom before disappearing into the night sky.

The next morning I awoke with a new feeling of hope, and I resolved to do my part to make it happen. I sat at my computer and began recording what I had seen as fast as my little fingers could type, as I waited impatiently for Albert to return, anxious to meet these mysterious friends who were helping us make the transition.

Chapter 6

Friends in High Places

Several days passed before Albert reappeared in my bedroom, grinning like a Cheshire cat. He told me he planned to take me to some of the ETs that Sophia had mentioned when we met with the Council of Wise Ones. Sophia had explained that several different ET civilizations were helping humans make the transition, and I was eager to learn more about them.

"Before you take me to meet the ETs, Albert, I would like a bit of background information about them," I began. "Who are they, and why can't they use their superior technology to fix what is wrong on Earth? Why don't they destroy all of our weapons of mass destruction, clean up all the pollution, and get rid of all the nasty political and religious leaders who promote conflict and violence? Wouldn't that be a lot easier than trusting humans to sort out their problems on their own?"

"All advanced life forms on the denser planes must observe the directive of noninterference, which means that they cannot directly interfere with the activities of another civilization unless it is necessary to prevent the destruction of a planet. They can help humans by giving guidance about living peacefully without negative emotions, and they can provide technical know-how when appropriate. But they cannot just wave a magic wand to fix everything that is wrong," Albert explained.

"So who established this rule of noninterference?" I responded.

"This directive was established by the Galactic Council that oversees all activities on the denser plane in your galaxy," Albert continued. "It is designed to ensure that all life forms have the opportunity to evolve on their own terms, even if it means that some civilizations will end up harming themselves and other life forms on their planet.

"All life on Earth, including humans, was seeded initially by ETs under the direction of the Galactic Council. They have monitored the progress of life on Earth from the very beginning, although they never knew for sure how it would play out. It was part of the grand experiment the Galactic Council conducted on all the planets that were capable of harboring life.

"Often the ETs have given humans help with their technological progress, teaching them agricultural husbandry and techniques for building large structures, as well as providing inspiration for inventions that have made life easier and safer for your people. The ETs have been helping humans ever since the first person walked on your planet, but they cannot cure all the problems that humans have created themselves.

"The ETs who have observed and visited Earth over the years came from many different planets in the Universe, and their civilizations were very diverse. Come with me and I will take you to one of their planets for a firsthand look."

Albert gently squeezed my arm and pointed toward Sagittarius. Once again all the stars disappeared, leaving nothing but the inky blackness of space. After a few seconds, the stars reappeared, and I saw that we were hovering near a bright orb that looked like our Sun, except it was a muted red in color. I noticed several planets circling this star as we swooped down toward the largest one.

As we got closer, I could see the colors that dominated this planet— royal blue, indigo, and purple. We continued our descent and touched down on its gravelly surface. The sky was a light pink, with its red sun appearing to be about three times the size of our sun when viewed from Earth. There were no plants or vegetation in sight, only gently undulating hills that spread out as far as the eye could see.

I followed Albert toward a small rectangular building hugging the surface. The little shack had no windows or other markings, just a doorway in the middle of the wall facing us. We entered this building and walked toward a large circular opening in the floor that led to a vertical tunnel beneath the surface. Albert clasped my hand as we stepped into the shaft and slowly floated down like feathers dropped from the sky.

We descended for several minutes before emerging into an immense underground cavern that housed a cluster of buildings. The pale yellow structures, which emanated soft white light from their walls, were either rectangular with flat roofs or circular and topped with domes, with round openings for windows and doors. The streets were paved with smooth bricks that gave off a gentle green glow.

I stood there transfixed, taking in the spectacle. We strolled down the main street toward a cluster of creatures standing in front of one of the larger buildings. They were not humanoid, but looked similar to spiders with piercing black eyes on a bulbous head that had two small antennae in constant motion. They were as tall as me and stood on four legs, with two more appendages that functioned like arms. Their bodies were black and shiny, almost metallic looking.

When we reached this group Albert addressed the entity in the center: "Greetings, Khepra, I brought you a visitor from Earth. I am taking him on a short tour of our galaxy, and I thought it would be good for him to meet you."

Khepra responded with a voice that sounded much like a human voice: "Welcome to our planet. Follow me and I will show you around."

"What is the name of your planet and where is it located?" I inquired.

"Our planet is called Xiron. It orbits a giant red star near the center of our galaxy," he replied.

"Why is the surface of your planet devoid of buildings or vegetation?" I asked.

"Our planet was covered with trees and other vegetation eons ago when our species lived on the surface. All of this was destroyed by excessive heat and radiation when our sun became a red giant. We now live exclusively in underground cities."

Khepra turned around and led us into the large structure behind him. We walked up to a railing inside and peered down at a massive circular room about twenty feet below us. There was a domed ceiling above us that emitted a soft white light. The room was filled with rows upon rows of horizontal circular monitors embedded in the floor, surrounded by dials and switches. Beside each monitor were two of the spider-like aliens who appeared to be watching the images on the screens.

Khepra explained that they used their advanced technology to observe all the planets in this section of the galaxy, which included Earth, to determine which ones were capable of harboring life. When their instruments detected favorable conditions for life, they reported this to the Galactic Council, who would then dispatch other ETs to travel to the planet for a close-up look. If the planet passed this physical inspection, the Galactic Council would initiate a program to seed it with life from other planets. Khepra advised that this had been the first step leading to the seeding of life on Earth many eons ago.

We were given a tour of the circular room, and Khepra did his best to explain how their instruments could detect and analyze planetary conditions many light years from Xiron. Although most of what he said was incomprehensible to me, I nodded my head from time to time like I understood everything. But I don't think I fooled Khepra, who was much too polite to expose my intellectual shortcomings.

When the tour was over, Albert and I bade farewell to Khepra and left the underground city. When we were high above Xiron, Albert pointed toward our sun and we returned to our rendezvous point high above Earth.

Before I could say anything, Albert announced that our next stop would be an ET spacecraft in a high orbit above Earth. I trailed Albert as we floated effortlessly toward a large silver globe in the distance. As we got closer, I could see it was a sphere about three stories tall with a smooth metallic surface punctuated by rows of round windows. We passed through the hull and stood on the edge of a brightly lit chamber teeming with activity. The walls of the room were lined with rectangular monitors that looked like large computer screens.

Dispersed throughout the room were several dozen humanoid beings who were busy punching keys below the monitors. They were about five feet tall, with hairless gray skin and arms and legs similar to humans. Their round heads were fitted with large oblong eyes, with small vertical slits where you would expect a nose and a horizontal slit for a mouth. They did not seem to notice us as they went about their business.

"These ETs are from the planet Nibiru that is hundreds of light years from Earth," Albert explained, "and this is one of the vehicles they use to travel to Earth. This spaceship is capable of faster-than-light travel, and their technology is vastly superior to anything found on Earth. They are here to observe your planet and provide help to your people to the extent possible."

Albert led me to a circular console in the center of the room. Standing in front of the console was an ET who seemed to be in charge of the activities in this room. Albert smiled at this ET and said: "Greetings, Rama, I brought a human in astral form to visit your ship and learn about your species and its history with Earth."

"Greetings to you, Albert, and to your companion from Earth. As you know, our species has been visiting Earth for thousands of years, even before it had any life. The Galactic Council sent us initially to confirm that Earth was suitable for life. When we advised them in the affirmative, the Council enlisted our help to begin the long process of seeding life on Earth. We started with primitive life forms from other planets in the galaxy, followed by more and more advanced life forms. Eventually, we seeded the planet with humans.

"Our mandate was to assist with the evolution and development of all forms of life on Earth, except we were not allowed to directly interfere with the events on the planet. Our assistance was much more subtle; we could teach humans new techniques to help them move forward and we could use our technology here and there to improve their way of life. For the most part, however, we were passive observers.

"Because of the noninterference directive, we were forced to sit on the sidelines and watch many of your highly evolved civilizations, like Atlantis and Lemuria, rise up to their glory days before collapsing. Tragically, these civilizations lost sight of their core values and succumbed to their negative emotions. They let the dark side of humanity triumph over love, and they paid the price. Every time this happened, the humans who survived the destruction had to start over again. It was difficult for us to watch these events, although we always held out the hope that the human experiment on Earth would eventually work out.

"Now humans have once again reached an advanced stage of development, a level which they can use as the launch pad to raise their vibrations and achieve a higher level of consciousness. And we have seen much progress in this regard in the last few decades as more and more humans are rejecting the dark side in favor of enlightenment. But not all humans are in the same place, and progress on this front seems unduly slow at times.

"The foremost concern we have is that humans have developed technology that is capable of destroying all life on Earth. Nuclear bombs, chemical and biological weapons, and other weapons of mass destruction are products of the dark side of humanity—the side that fosters fear, anger, hate, and greed.

"We have the capability to destroy all of your weapons, but we are not allowed to do so. The shift to enlightenment must be done by humans themselves, with a little help from their friends. Ever since humans first split the atom during World War II, Earth has attracted the attention of many other ET races who are now watching the activities on Earth. They too cannot directly interfere with events on Earth, although they are also working quietly behind the scenes to help humans. All the ET species have worked closely with the Council of Wise Ones who have been coordinating all the activities to encourage humans to discard the darkness and embrace the light. And the pace and intensity of these efforts has increased markedly in recent years.

"We are in the middle of a full-court press with humanity because the time for action is upon us. We are determined to use every effort we can muster to ensure that your civilization does not destroy itself, but we need all the help we can get.

"We carefully monitor all activity on your planet to detect situations that might lead to disputes or conflicts that have the potential to escalate out of control. In these cases, our goal is to scale back the hostilities with a program of intense telepathic thoughts beamed at those humans who are capable of calming the discord and spreading the peace. This has not always worked in the past, but we continue to improve our techniques to target the right people with our plea to discard fear and anger and embrace love and compassion.

"Right now, as in the past, with the use of our advanced technology, some members of our race are living on Earth disguised as humans. You have likely encountered these pseudo-humans many times in the past without being aware of their true identities. Their mission is to exert a positive influence on the humans around them through their words and actions so that more and more humans will shun the darkness and welcome the light.

"As well, we have enlisted some of your people, directly or by telepathy, to communicate our message of hope to other humans via inter-personal contacts and broad dissemination through various media channels. This is why Albert brought you here. We want you to communicate our aspirations for humanity as part of our master plan. You are just one small cog in a very large wheel—but every little bit helps."

"I wish you could interfere directly, but I understand the rules you must follow," I lamented. "I guess humans will have to muddle their way through this the hard way."

I waved farewell to Rama as Albert and I glided out of the ship to hover in our usual rendezvous spot high above Earth.

"From what I have seen so far, Albert, we still need a lot of help on our path to enlightenment. Can you tell me more about how the ETs have been helping humans? Is it working according to plan?"

"First of all, the ETs have provided humans with information and techniques at crucial points in their development. The ETs hoped to make life easier for humans so people would not need to devote all of their time finding food and shelter for their families. They knew it would be difficult for humans to expand their consciousness if they had to struggle every day just to survive. Starving humans are not able to sit quietly to listen to Spirit, since their overriding focus is to find food to alleviate their hunger pangs.

"So from time to time throughout your history the ETs have helped humans find new ways to raise their standard of living. They taught humans how to grow their own food, become better hunters and foragers, and make better tools and hunting weapons. With guidance from the ETs, humans learned how to organize their societies so that individuals could specialize in a trade or profession and barter with other humans for food and essentials. Hundreds of your noteworthy inventions, like the printing press, microscopes, penicillin, electric lights, and telephones, to name a few, were inspired by your off-world benefactors.

"Historically, most of this assistance has been very subtle. Quite often, as Rama mentioned, these aliens would disguise themselves as humans so they could be of service without being conspicuous. Often they would send telepathic messages to gifted people to inspire the development of groundbreaking inventions that boosted your technology to the next level. Occasionally they landed in their starships and used their superior technology to move large stones to build pyramids and other massive structures. Several of these encounters have been described in your holy books as miracles performed by angels.

"Unfortunately, some of the help humans got from the ETs was used for the wrong purpose—to enable a few men to subjugate and kill other humans to satisfy their thirst for money and power. Since the ETs were not allowed to directly intervene, they could only stand by and watch the bloodshed with dismay. They still have high hopes, however, that humans will eventually make the quantum leap up to the next level."

"Please tell me about the spaceship we just left, Albert. Are these ships ever seen by humans? Are they the UFOs that we read about in magazines and books?"

"They are sometimes visible to humans, but only when the ETs choose it to be so," Albert responded. "They can use cloaking devices to make their craft invisible to radar and the human eye. Sometimes they choose to be visible to people on your planet, as it is their way of gently making you aware of their presence before they engage in full and open contact with everyone."

"What about the people who claim to have been abducted and taken aboard alien ships? Are these abductions real and have the ETs been responsible?" I inquired.

"The so-called abductions have been carried out by your alien visitors for centuries. There is nothing malevolent about these events—all of them occur without any harm to the abductees and only for the purpose of studying the human anatomy and implanting communication devices. Their intention is only to help these people carry out their life purpose for the benefit of all humans. If the ETs wanted to harm humans they could have wiped them out long ago. You have to trust that they have benevolent intentions and are proceeding with their own timetable. Some day in the not-too-distant future they will reveal themselves to everyone on Earth, but until then they will continue to operate discretely," Albert responded patiently.

"Why haven't they made open contact with all humans? Surely this would inspire people to see the light and change their ways," I offered.

"The ETs are following instructions from the Galactic Council, which believes that open contact with humans would not be a good idea at this time. The Council is concerned that most humans are not yet ready to accept that Earth has been visited by alien civilizations with superior technology, and knowledge of this could lead to anxiety, social disruption, and even panic. Some humans might think their governments were weak and ineffectual in comparison, thereby breeding contempt and disrespect for secular authority. The Council is monitoring the situation carefully, and they will allow open contact when they think humans are able to handle it gracefully."

"All humans should be grateful for the help we have received from the ETs, and I certainly hope it continues, even if it is subtle and discreet," I observed. "But what about the good souls on the Spirit Side? How they are helping us?"

"As Sophia mentioned, the Council of Wise Ones has been active in a number of ways," Albert responded. "It has been actively recruiting highly evolved souls from all over the Universe to incarnate on Earth to help humans make the shift before they self-destruct. Some of these souls are Masters who have incarnated on Earth to encourage humans to embrace love and spiritual enlightenment. Often these advanced souls do not remember where they came from or anything about the missions they undertook, although they are nonetheless helping your cause by setting good examples for other humans to follow.

"Over the past few decades, the Council has been increasing the pace of its dispatches sent to Earth, with the hope that these messages will be understood and accepted by those humans who have been selected to spread the word. Their guidance has been sent through many different channels throughout the world, including psychics and mediums, as more and more humans are recognizing their psychic abilities and using this talent to help others connect with Spirit. In recent years there has been a noticeable increase in the number of people who have reported out-of-body trips to the Spirit Side when they were deemed to be clinically dead. Near-death experiences have always been part of human life, although historically most people have been reluctant to talk about their experiences for fear of being ridiculed. Now more people are willing to openly discuss their out-of-body excursions as a way of providing comfort and hope to others. These people are allowed to retain the memories of their astral journeys so they can change their lives for the better and help others to do the same.

"And in a few cases, like my direct communication with you, the Council has chosen humans on Earth to promulgate its messages through books, lectures, Internet postings, and spiritual gatherings, which is intended to ensure that everyone will have the opportunity to understand what they must do to enhance their spiritual enlightenment."

"Thank you, Albert, for taking me to see Xiron and the ET spacecraft and for your insights on the contributions the ETs have made in our development. It is good to know we have friends in high places."

Albert signaled it was time for me to return home. So I followed him down through the clouds toward my house and back into my bedroom, where my body was still in bed, snuggled under the covers in a peaceful sleep. But before I slid back into the physical world, Albert promised me he would be back soon to answer all my questions as we continued our intrepid exploration for the truth.

Chapter 7

Taking the Next Step

My life was beginning to seem a little dull after all the adventures I had with Albert. Writing a book was not nearly as exciting as tripping through the Universe. I wished Albert could write it for me—it would be so much easier. And it would be wonderful if I could just explore the cosmos with Albert and forget about all the problems on Earth. After all, humans had gotten themselves into this predicament, and they had no one else to blame. But naturally I have a soft spot in my heart for humans despite their faults. All of my family and friends are humans, and I want my grandchildren to grow up in a better place—a planet where all humans and creatures live together in peace and harmony without abusing Mother Earth.

But wishful thinking was not going to get us there. And spending too much time contemplating the future was as futile as dwelling on the past. So I did what Albert expected of me and continued the tedious task of writing about what I had seen so far on my astral exploits. Luckily, everything I had seen with Albert was vividly etched in my memory, more so than anything else I could recall from my past.

As I reflected on my nightly escapades with Albert, I wondered about the next step for humans. Although we had made a lot of progress in the last few decades, there was still too much pollution, too much abuse of other creatures, and too many humans suffering from maltreatment and neglect. We still have an excess of fear, anger, and greed, and not enough love. Humans must become better at sharing our resources and finding ways to curb crime and violent conflicts. And we must learn to accept all other humans regardless of their nationality, religion, or skin color.

After several uneventful days following my visit to the ET spacecraft, I pined for Albert's return and the chance for another out-of-body adventure. I began to think he had gone on vacation, although I suspected his whole life was one big vacation. It was definitely good work if you could get it.

Albert eventually made his appearance once again in the dead of the night with his sparkling eyes and toothy grin. I was anxious to see what he had in store for me, so I quickly slid out of my sleeping body and followed him up into the darkness of night until we paused at the usual gathering point high above Earth.

Before Albert could speak, I vented my frustrations and concerns about the dire prospects for human civilization on my planet. When I finished my harangue, Albert tried his best to cheer me up.

"Although the picture you paint seems very grim, you must remember that human civilization in this go-around has made a quantum leap from the fear, desperation, and depravity of the Dark Ages. In the last fifty years significant advances have been made in the developed world in respect of human rights, the sharing of wealth and resources, and the curtailment of animal abuse. At the same time there has been global recognition of the problems caused by the pollution of your environment, and many countries have been working diligently to reduce all harmful discharges.

"In the past few decades, more and more humans have become spiritually aware of who they are and what is important for their journeys on Earth. Many have adopted a standard of love, hope, and forgiveness instead of the guilt and fear fostered by most organized religions. There has been a new awareness in some people that they are not separate entities but are connected to one another and to everything else in the Universe. And when they cast aside the illusions of separation, the need to judge other people for their actions or status in life disappears, along with the impulse to be fearful and distrustful of those people who are different in some way.

"The revelations you described in your first book are truths that more and more humans are ready to accept as part of their spiritual development. You may have already noticed the huge increase in the number of people today who are spiritually aware, compared to thirty years ago. All of these factors have encouraged many humans to adopt new spiritual paradigms that help them understand the purpose of their journeys on Earth.

"Try to remember what it was like thirty or forty years ago and reflect on the progress that has been made. Do you think your first book, *Dancing on a Stamp*, would have been published or read by anyone in the seventies? For that matter, do you think you would have written this book back then? More likely than not you would have kept everything to yourself for fear of ridicule from friends and coworkers.

"As you are aware, humanity still has a ways to go before all of the remaining negatives have been extinguished. Do not despair, however, because help is on the way from your allies. The Galactic Council, the Council of Wise Ones, and the ETs will continue their efforts to help all humans make the transition to spiritual enlightenment.

"Everyone can help the cause by heeding some simple advice: Before reacting to the events in your life, take a moment to pause and reflect on how your words or actions might affect those people around you. Try to remember what it was like as a soul on the Spirit Side where negative emotions and actions do not exist, and where everyone loves everyone else unconditionally. Then ask yourself what your soul would want you to do in any situation. Reject the temptation to judge others or react with condensation or anger, and let your heart be filled with love for all the people and creatures on your planet.

"Bestow your smiles freely and warmly on others so they will smile back at you. Laugh often with others, not at them. Be kind to someone at least once every day, with joy in your heart, and strive to help others find their way on the path to spiritual awareness. Spread your message of love and hope wherever you go and always set a good example for others to follow. Understand that every little bit helps no matter how insignificant it may seem. Humans need to quiet their minds, listen to their guidance, and live their lives accordingly. With the help of more and more people pulling together, I am confident that humanity will rise up to the challenge and move on to the next level."

"Thank you, Albert, for the pep talk. I wish you could go on a worldwide television broadcast to tell all humans what you just told me. It would make everyone's job so much easier."

"You know I cannot do that. Humans must work their way through this the hard way without divine intervention. No one told you that life on Earth would be easy, and yet you still decided to incarnate on this planet with full knowledge of the obstacles you would face. You need to stop looking for the easy way out and get on with your job."

"I knew you were going to say that, but I had to try anyway."

"It never hurts to ask. Do you have any more questions before we head off for your next trek?"

I nodded my head and pulled from my pocket a sheet of paper filled with handwritten questions. Albert groaned a little and then braced himself for my onslaught.

Chapter 8

Piercing the Gossamer Veil

"I have plenty more questions for you, Albert, but I feel like a mosquito at a nudist camp: I know what to do, but I hardly know where to start. It seems to me that humans must first get their own houses in order before they can hope to encourage others to do the same. So I would like to ask for your advice on how individual humans can expand their consciousness as the first step in the quest to make positive changes to our civilization.

"Many people who read *Dancing on a Stamp* have told me they would love to communicate with their spirit guides like I do with you, Albert. I would like to help them out, although I have no idea what to tell them. When you first appeared to me I did not know who you were, and you initiated the conversation without any special effort on my part. Can you give me a few tips on spirit communication that I can pass on to everyone else who wants to connect with their guides?"

"The communication we have had was planned before you were born when you were preparing your Life Plan, even though you do not remember it," Albert replied. "It is not a commonplace form of communication and is not something that everyone can achieve.

"I am communicating directly with you for a special reason. Our goal on the Spirit Side is to disseminate inspirational messages to people on Earth to help them understand why they are having a journey in a human body and to encourage them to reject guilt and fear in favor of love, hope, and forgiveness. I am part of a much larger effort by Spirit to encourage humans to expand their spiritual awareness. Our efforts in this regard have paid off; we have noticed that more and more humans have come to understand that they are spiritual beings having a human incarnation. This knowledge helps them embrace their spirituality and reject negative reactions to the experiences they encounter during their lives on Earth.

"As I mentioned before, you were chosen to be one of our messengers, and that is why I made this direct contact with you. We knew you were capable of writing books about our revelations, and our goal was to channel the information to you in a way you could easily understand and pass on to others. You have enjoyed a good start in that role; however, we have many more insights to send your way."

"What about the people that have not been contacted by their guides," I responded. "Is it possible to teach them how to communicate with souls on the Spirit Side?"

"The first step to better communication with your soul and guides is learning to live in the present moment by focusing on what is happening right now. You must rid yourself of all unnecessary thoughts about the past—what you did yesterday, last week, or last year—while retaining only the lessons you learned from your past experiences. Dwelling on the past sucks energy from your being and it serves no useful purpose. Thinking about the past often generates negative emotions—like regret, guilt, and anger—which prevents you from concentrating on what is really important.

"Contemplating the future is equally distracting. While it is necessary to do some basic planning to ensure an orderly life, spending too much time worrying about the future also drains your energy and generates other negative emotions, like fear and anxiety.

"As I pointed out before, the past and the future are anomalies of your planet, where you see time as a linear progression. On the Spirit Side, linear time does not exist, and everything that has happened in the 'past' or that will happen in the 'future' is all happening in the present moment.

"To live in the present you must ditch your thoughts about the past and the future, which clutter your mind each and every day. You cannot easily hear messages from your guides if your mind is clogged with random thoughts about what you did yesterday or what may happen to you next week. Imagine you are in a room crowded with fifty people who are all talking to you at the same time. There is one person at the back of the room who you really want to hear, but you have great difficulty discerning what this person is saying because of all the noise. In order to hear this person you must first clear everybody else out of the room. Then you will be able to understand the only message that is really important to you."

"That is easier said than done," I countered. "How can I expect to clear the clutter from my mind when I have become used to living this way? This state of mind seems natural to me and focusing on the present moment is not easy to achieve."

"No one said it would be easy. It takes determination and lots of practice to win this battle. This is one of the biggest challenges that humans face, but success will be very rewarding. Humans have developed many different techniques to help them quiet the mind and live in the present moment, and most of which rely on some form of meditation. There is no magical path to follow to achieve the desired results; the right course of action is the one that works best for each person.

"Take a few meditation courses, join a meditation group, or read books on how to meditate. Find something that works for you and then stick with it. And then you must practice and practice until you reach the blissful state of unity with the Universe. This will help you to hear all the whispers from your soul and understand the guidance you receive from beyond the veil."

Although I agreed with Albert about using meditation to communicate with Spirit, I wanted to find an alternative for those people who found it difficult to meditate. I wondered if there was an easier way for humans to connect with souls on the Spirit Side.

"What about psychics and mediums, Albert? Do these people have special communication links with souls on the Spirit Side? Can I hear from my guides through one of these channels?"

"Many psychics and mediums are able peer through the veil and communicate with souls on the Spirit Side," Albert replied. "They can channel messages from your guides and from loved ones who have crossed over to the Other Side. The clarity of these transmissions varies greatly as it is directly related to the skill and experience of the psychic or medium. And the content of the channeled information is always restricted to glimpses of the whole picture to ensure no one gets the detailed blueprint of the life that lies ahead of them."

"Before you lead me away on my next adventure, I would like to go back home to explore this type of spirit communication in greater depth," I responded. Albert nodded his agreement and led me back to my bedroom where I slipped quietly back into my body.

The next morning I decided to gather more information about people with highly developed psychic abilities. Although I had already met a number of psychics and mediums, especially after *Dancing on a Stamp* was published, I did not know any who lived close to my home. So I searched the Internet for psychics in my city and found one that came highly recommended.

Cassandra was an attractive lady in her late thirties with a warm and enchanting smile. She invited me to sit in her studio while she popped my cassette tape into her recorder. Then she began the reading by describing my background, my career, and all the frustrations in my life. She knew I had been a lawyer for most of my life and was now a writer, and I was in the midst of writing my second book. (We had never met before, and I had not given her any details about me before the session started.) She also disclosed some intimate information about me and my family—things I had never revealed to anyone before.

At this point I knew she was for real; she could not have guessed these details with such accuracy. She went on to answer my questions about personal matters that would affect me in the future, some of which have already come true. When the reading was over, I lingered to ask Cassandra about her background.

She told me she had been psychic since she was a little girl. From an early age she could see and hear things her parents and siblings could not see or hear, although she did not know where these visions and sounds came from or what they meant. She kept these strange occurrences to herself for the most part because her parents liked to dismiss them as products of a vivid imagination. It wasn't until she was in her late twenties that she realized these images and sounds were coming from spirits on the other side of the veil, and she began to focus on becoming better at discerning these messages.

Then about eight years ago, after consulting with other psychics to hone her skills, she began to do readings for other people. She found success early on and has always received very positive feedback from her clients.

She explained that typically the spirits who come through in a reading give her a mixture of images, symbols, and verbal thought messages. She knew it was not her job to interpret or understand the messages, but merely to pass them on to her clients. The spirits who come through to her in a session are not always the same, and they often do not identify themselves.

Cassandra did not know how she came to have this talent, but she surmised that her enhanced psychic abilities likely resulted from a quirk in her genetics. She believed that most people have some psychic abilities, although they don't always recognize them for what they are.

Cassandra felt she had a duty to use her special talents to help other people, and she was happy to do so. Although the messages she passes on to her clients were often helpful to people who were struggling with important life decisions, she knew Spirit would never give anyone the complete road map for their lives. She believed the messages from Spirit were only intended to provide a few hints about the right path to follow—a shortcut for those people who were stuck in a rut and needed a little extra help to move forward.

Before I left, Cassandra cautioned me that not everyone who claims to be a psychic is the real thing, and the best way to find a genuine psychic was through recommendations from satisfied clients.

I thanked Cassandra for her help and left her studio. Even though she had been helpful in my quest for information, I wished she could have given me more guidance on what my future would bring. But I knew this would never happen in this difficult school called Earth.

The next night after my reading with Cassandra, Albert returned and signaled for me to follow him to our usual rendezvous point high above Earth. I sensed that Albert had something to show me, so I waited quietly for him to lead the way.

Albert told me he knew about my visit with Cassandra, and he thought it would be useful for me to see the negative side of visions from the spirit realm. While psychics and mediums are able to handle the flow of messages from Spirit without any major disruptions to their lives, some people are not able to cope with this influx and their personal lives can become unraveled.

I followed Albert down toward a city in the eastern seaboard of the United States that I could not recognize, and we dropped through the roof of a large rectangular building that was around ten stories tall. Albert explained that we were in a mental hospital where people with severe mental handicaps (in the opinion of the medical establishment) were institutionalized for their protection and for the good of society. We entered the room of a patient in her mid-thirties who was sitting quietly in her chair, staring at the wall. Her hair was tousled and uncombed, and she had a faraway look in her eyes.

"Her name is Judy, and she was admitted here two years ago after being diagnosed with severe schizophrenia," Albert explained. "She has a husband and two children, aged seven and ten, who come to visit her every Sunday. Her husband, who loves her dearly, has found it very difficult to deal with her situation and raise their children as a single parent. Her children do not understand why she must stay in this hospital. They miss her a lot and pray she will return home soon."

"Why did you bring me here, Albert? What did you want me to learn?"

"I wanted to show you an example of the tragic fallout that can result when people are unable to cope with the stream of images and messages they receive from beyond the veil. In a lot of cases, medical professionals contribute to the problem because they refuse to accept any explanation that falls outside of the established guidelines for mental health. All too often they misdiagnose a patient's mental condition and prescribe treatment in a mental hospital, which often leaves them in perpetual state of sedation, unable to interact normally with staff or family visitors. And this reinforces the doctors' view that the patient would not be able to function normally outside of the institution.

"The real tragedy is that in many of these situations the patient in not mentally dysfunctional, but is actually operating at a level far above what is considered normal for humans. Judy is a good example, as she has been a gifted psychic since she was a small child. Early on she could see and hear people that others could not perceive because they were spirits from beyond the veil. Judy could not understand why her parents could not see these people who had become regular visitors in her life. Her parents dismissed these visions as the product of an overactive imagination and often scolded her for making up stories. Judy soon learned it was best to not mention these special people to anyone.

"These spirits continued to be a part of her life, and she grew to enjoy their companionship. The downside to this was that she spent less and less time with other children and more and more time by herself conversing with her spirit friends. These visitations continued through her teens, and Judy often received prescient information about future events that she sometimes revealed to her family and friends. She stopped sharing this information when she realized that the accuracy of her predictions frightened her parents.

"Judy got married in her twenties and gave birth to two lovely children. She was a loving and devoted wife and mother, but she never mentioned her contact with the spirits to her husband.

"Then about three years ago, Judy started seeing things that were new to her. She saw glimpses of other dimensions through an opening in the veil that shields humans from the other realities that exist all around us. The vistas she saw in these other dimensions were often bewildering and mind-boggling, and she had to struggle to keep things in perspective. Ultimately, she had to tell her husband about her visions because she could no longer keep them bottled up inside.

"This caused problems for Judy because her husband, who was a kind and understanding man, found her visions to be strange and unbelievable. And when Judy continued to describe the things and places she saw in these other dimensions, her husband became very concerned—especially when she brought her children into the loop. Finally, in order to please her husband, Judy agreed to see a psychiatrist, even though she knew she was perfectly sane.

"You can guess what happened next. After several visits the psychiatrist recommended that Judy be admitted to the psychiatric ward of the local hospital for observation. When she continued to 'hallucinate,' she was admitted to this institution and given sedatives every day. Judy still sees past the veil, although she has lost all interest in her life on Earth as a result of the sedation. She doesn't think about her family anymore as she is now totally immersed in her new world. That is why she just stares at the wall—she is enjoying her adventures in the other dimensions and no longer wants to focus on the harsh realities of life in this institution."

"This is a very tragic story, Albert. Does this happen often?"

"Unfortunately, it does. Medical science does not recognize things they do not understand or cannot examine in a laboratory. Anything that does not fit neatly into their narrow view of the world is dismissed outright. So instead of delving into the possibility that Judy was really peering through the veil to view life in other dimensions, they found it much easier and more comforting to diagnose her with chronic schizophrenia and lock her up in this hospital. Judy is only one example of thousands of other patients whose paranormal visions are mistaken for mental illness. It demonstrates an unfortunate human tendency to be fearful of what they do not understand. A few hundred years ago, people who acted abnormally like this would have been branded as witches and burned at the stake or tortured and killed for being in league with the devil. In your modern society they usually get locked up in mental institutions."

"What can we do about this, Albert? How can we prevent this from happening to other people?"

"Through education and revelation, my friend. You must disseminate this information to those people who can change the system. Someday medical science will understand that people like Judy have a special gift that should be respected and not feared."

Then we left Judy, and Albert guided me back to my bedroom, promising to return the next night to take me on another cosmic adventure.

Chapter 9

Thoughts Are Energy

The next morning after our visit to the mental hospital I tried to prioritize my questions for Albert, since I did not know how long he would put up with my insatiable curiosity. I recalled one of our earlier conversations when Albert told me thoughts are like waves of energy that fan out from our minds and affect all other energy and mass in the Universe. And similar thoughts emanating from many minds can combine to form an even more powerful wave of energy. Given my Christian upbringing, I wondered if thinking was the same as praying.

The leaders of organized religions have always extolled the virtues of prayer as an appeal to God to provide relief from pain and suffering or to achieve a goal—like passing an exam, finding a good job, or connecting with an ideal mate. In this paradigm, our thoughts are not instruments of change themselves but are merely a way of communicating our desires to God, who has the power to deliver the desired result if he sees fit. This is in keeping with their belief that God controls and manipulates all the events in our lives, and we must pray to God to get the results we want. And these religious leaders were happy to demonstrate how to pray effectively in order to reach God, which usually involved attending a place of worship on a regular basis and following the rules established by these holy men.

As disclosed in *Dancing on a Stamp*, Albert dismissed this belief as an invention of the holy men; it was a tool they could use to control the masses. Albert was clear that the Source does not manipulate events on Earth or interfere with the free-will actions of humans, which means that prayer and worship will not prod the Source to interfere with our lives.

So if our thoughts will not cause the Source to act on our behalf, how do thoughts affect our reality on Earth? Are all thoughts equal in force or are some thoughts more powerful than others?

When Albert returned that night I posed these questions to him, and he responded thoughtfully.

"Thoughts affect your reality because they create your perception about the events you encounter every day. When things happen to you, your mind will perceive them to be either good or bad, sending out thoughts that will create either positive or negative emotions. If you prefer to live a happy life, then you need to focus your thoughts on being happy regardless of what you encounter. However, if you let negative thoughts rule the day you will spend most of your life mired in gloom and despair.

"Your thoughts can also affect your reality when you communicate with other people. Humans can consciously and unconsciously project their thoughts toward others to persuade them to choose a certain course of action. Some people are very adept at selling things or convincing others to act in accordance with their wishes. They are able to do so mainly because they can beam powerful thoughts, often unconsciously, to persuade others to do what they want. The people who receive these thoughts often respond without being consciously aware of these thought projections. Similarly, thoughts can influence a recruiter to hire you for the job, persuade an art judge that your painting deserves first place, or convince someone that you would make a perfect life mate. In these situations, the reality of both the sender and receiver of these thoughts has been affected by the decisions that are made in response.

"Thoughts can also communicate concepts, ideas, and feelings. One identical twin often will know what the other twin is thinking and feeling, even if they are hundreds of miles apart. Couples who have been living together for many years have been known to come up with identical solutions to a problem without prior discussion and to finish each other's sentences during a conversation.

"Because thoughts are energy, they can manipulate other energy and matter in the Universe. A focused thought is more powerful than a scattered thought, much like a laser beam of coherent light waves is more powerful than the incoherent beam from a flashlight. Not all of your thoughts on Earth that seek a particular outcome are manifested because they are often canceled out by conflicting thoughts from other people. On the Spirit Side, there are no conflicting thoughts and every thought is manifested as soon as it is expressed.

"And when your thoughts are in direct conflict with the goals sought by your soul, your desires will be put on hold until your soul is satisfied that what you seek will not send you on a wrong trajectory. If you visualize that you will own a red Ferrari, your soul may resist this desire because you might drive too fast and become injured in an accident—an event your soul does not want to experience. The unfortunate reality on Earth is that your desires will not likely be fulfilled, no matter how often you send positive affirmations out to the Universe, unless your soul is onside.

"Repetition, however, can make your thoughts more effective on the Earth plane. Since every thought is a wave of energy, repeated waves of like energy can merge to become much more powerful than an isolated thought. The most effective way to achieve the results you desire is by repeating positive affirmations and visualizations over and over until you get what you want."

"What do I do if my soul does not want me to manifest a certain desire?" I pondered. "How can I still achieve my goal? Is there any way for me to convince my soul that my yearnings should be fulfilled? And for that matter, how can I know if my soul is with me or against me when I project my thoughts to the Universe?"

Albert sighed gently and responded: "You can never know for sure what your soul wants you to achieve, because you do not have access to the Life Plan your soul prepared before you were born. Your Life Plan, however, is not etched in stone; your soul can change it as your life proceeds, and it will do so if the events in your life warrant a change. If you really want something, send out the most focused thoughts you can muster and repeat them over and over. Your soul will be influenced by your thoughts, and it may be possible to get your soul onside with a concerted effort. If you can do this, your thoughts will be manifested much sooner because both you and your soul will be sending the same message to the Universe."

This discussion about the power of thought reminded me of the conversation Albert and I had about the Law of Attraction when I was writing *Dancing on a Stamp*. He had explained then that the Law of Attraction did not always work on Earth because of the shortage of some material goods on the denser planes or because our desires were not supported by our souls.

Given all of this, I wondered how so many best-selling books about the Law of Attraction could take the position that it works every time.

As always, Albert had an interesting response: "The authors of the books you mention are doing whatever they can to sell lots of books, and the best way to do this is to assure the reader that the Law of Attraction always works. So they cite numerous examples of how it has worked in the past for them or for other people, which provides hope and inspiration to the reader. What they neglect to mention is that for every situation where it has worked, there were ninety-nine other cases where it didn't work. They deliberately mention only the successes, never the failed attempts. So they provide a distorted picture on how thoughts can be manifested on your planet.

"This approach is understandable, since no one wants to hear about unfulfilled desires. Everybody wants to read about the happy times when someone's positive thinking reaped wonderful rewards. It provides a ray of hope that the readers can also get whatever they want simply by following the guidance in these books.

"Unfortunately, they find out soon enough that their thoughts are not always manifested in the magical way described in these books, and they must continue their search for the secret to living a happier life. It is much like the people who try out one fad diet after another searching for an easy way to lose weight and keep it off.

"But don't take this the wrong way. It is always useful have positive thoughts in your life. Negative thoughts can drag you down and slow your progress. Positive thoughts will make you feel better, and you will be a happier person because of it, even if all of your wishes are not fulfilled. If you recognize this, you will not be disappointed when your desires are not fulfilled, and you will cherish those occasions when your thoughts deliver the results you hoped for."

Now I understood why I have never won the lottery—it was my higher self holding me back. (Or maybe it was because I never bought lottery tickets.)

As Albert waited patiently for my next question, I told him I was curious about miracles, since I had noticed recently that many books and Facebook posts claimed that miracles will happen to anyone who truly believes in them. That seemed a bit too easy; I had always thought that miracles required some form of divine intervention. Although I expected Albert would be able to shed some light on this subject, I wanted to reflect on what I knew about miracles before springing my questions on him. And just maybe Albert could arrange for a few miracles to be tossed my way.

Chapter 10

Everyday Miracles

The word miracle is defined as "a surprising and welcome event that is not explicable by natural or scientific laws and is considered to be divine," and the term has been used by humans for centuries, including dozens of references in the Bible. It is common today for people to believe miracles are created by God in his discretion, often in response to prayers from his faithful followers.

Miracles are events or actions that deliver wonderful, inexplicable results to those who receive them, such as a terminal cancer patient making a full recovery. Events that defy the odds but are clearly explainable under our natural laws, such as winning the lottery, are not true miracles even if it may seem like one to the person with the winning ticket.

The key element of a miracle is that scientists cannot offer a plausible explanation for what happened based on the laws of nature as they know them at the time. Thus, events that are thought to be miraculous in one era may be common occurrences in a subsequent period. A hundred years ago, watching a baseball game or a concert on a glass panel in your home would have been miraculous. As Walter C. Clarke said: "Any sufficiently advanced technology is indistinguishable from magic"—or from miracles, for that matter.

Most of the miracles Jesus performed, like multiplying fish and loaves of bread, turning water into wine, and walking on water, have not yet been duplicated by science, even though they might be someday. And it may not be science that finds a way to replicate these miracles; the answer may come from ordinary humans who have learned how to utilize the full power of their brains.

I have always been intrigued by the miracles attributed to Jesus in the scriptures. Turning water into wine and raising people from the dead are amazing feats, indeed. But I wondered why Jesus did not use his powers to save himself from a painful death on the cross?

This led to the inevitable question for Albert: Are miracles caused by the direct intervention of the Source, or are they created by humans who have learned to manifest their desires with powerful, focused thoughts?

As usual, Albert had an insightful answer for me: "Miracles do not originate from the Source because, as I have said before, the Source does not control or manipulate events on Earth. Historically, most religions have attributed all miracles to God as his answer to prayers from the faithful. They took this position because they had no other plausible explanation for the miracles, and it enhanced their vision of God as the Supreme Being who could do wondrous things for those people who worshiped him and followed his rules. It reinforced their teachings that everyone should pray often and worship God on a regular basis.

"The miracles you mentioned were actually created by humans who were able to focus their thoughts in a powerful way to achieve results that science could not explain. They were merely harnessing forces in the Universe that have always been available to those humans who knew how to utilize them. Since most people are not aware of this energy, they assume all miracles result from divine intervention.

"Jesus was a notable example of a human who had learned to unleash the powerful energy of the Universe to perform his miracles. There are many other examples in your history: Moses parting the Red Sea and the sun and moon standing still for Joshua are two notable examples. And there have been countless other miracles throughout the ages, undocumented for the most part, which resulted in paraplegics learning to walk again, infertile women conceiving children, blind people regaining their sight, and clinically dead patients making full recoveries.

"Most humans do not realize how powerful they can be if they tap into the energy of the Universe, and they tend to give credit to God for all miracles. On the Spirit Side, thought creation is very powerful, and every soul knows how to use thoughts to manifest the things they want. But things are not that easy on Earth, where most humans have not yet learned how to focus their thoughts to achieve the results they desire.

"Someday humans will be able to walk on water and turn water into wine, but they must first raise their level of consciousness and increase their vibratory rates. This will allow them greater utilization of the human mind, and what you would consider a miracle today will be commonplace in the future."

"It would be wonderful if I could turn water into wine," I said wistfully, "But what about water into whisky?"

"Don't push your luck. If you continue to annoy me, I will turn you into a toad."

"Can you do that?"

"I can, but I won't—because I promised the Council I would not do anything to improve your appearance," Albert retorted, wearing his mischievous grin.

I thought about flipping him the bird, but I was afraid he might disappear in a huff, and I had many more questions for him. So I bit my tongue and continued.

"How can I learn to use more of my brain, Albert? What do I need to do to achieve this enhanced state of consciousness?"

"You need to quiet your mind and focus your thoughts. You must rid yourself of your negative emotions in every aspect of your life. You must not dwell on the past, and you must forgive yourself for all the mistakes you have made. Then you should forgive everyone who has ever caused you any harm, which must be an unconditional forgiveness without the expectation of anything in return. Finally, you must stop contemplating the future and worrying about the bad things that may happen to you or your family. It is important that you learn to live in the present moment and have faith that everything in your life will unfold as it should.

"You must learn to live your life with this in mind so that you will not hate those people who cause you harm or become angry about the events in your life that do not go according to your plan. Do not judge or fear other people because they have a different religion or way of life. Live your life like you truly understand we are all part of the Source—connected to one another and everything else in the Universe—and discard your illusions of separation.

"When you are able to do all of these things consistently, you will discover how to focus the energy of your thoughts to manifest your desires, and you too will be capable of spawning miracles every day."

"I hear what you are saying, Albert, although to do this is easier said than done. You have already been a huge influence on my life since that day long ago when you confronted me on the street. I only wish you could wave your magic wand and turn me into the kind of person you just described. It would be so much easier," I lamented.

"I think you already know the answer to that request," Albert retorted. "I could arrange for this to happen, but I won't because it would not be in your best interests. You will just have to slug it out on Earth like everyone else, with no special favors. You will understand why this is so when you pass over to the Spirit Side and you fully understand the reality of the life on Earth."

This was the answer I had expected from Albert, although it never hurts to try. So I decided to move on to my next question: "I have one final query about miracles. You mentioned that Jesus had learned to utilize the energy of the Universe to perform his miracles. Why did he not use this ability to save himself from crucifixion? Was he not capable of removing the nails from his hands and feet and levitating down from the cross?"

"Jesus certainly could have saved himself from the cross, but that wasn't something he wanted or needed to do. He was not afraid of death because he knew who he was and where he would go after his physical body died. He let himself be crucified since he believed this was the best way to make a powerful statement to humanity—that he could resurrect himself from the dead and ascend into Heaven. He intended that his death and resurrection would be the miraculous catalyst for the start of a new religion that would help humanity start down the road to enlightenment. And the Christian Church that arose from his death has had a huge impact on humans, even though it was hijacked to a certain extent by the holy men who followed Jesus.

Although Jesus had good intentions, the Church he originated strayed off course after his death because of the free-will actions of the religious leaders that followed him.

"Now humans are once again in need of a boost to take them to the next level. They need a catalyst to spur them to make significant changes in the way they interact with other humans, the creatures on your planet, and Mother Earth herself. Except this time it won't be one messiah leading them to the Promised Land; it will be many people from all over the world who will work quietly behind the scenes to help humans make the transition. No new religion will be created; instead there will be a universal, almost imperceptible, expansion of consciousness without any one person being the focal point. All of our messengers who are spreading the word about spiritual enlightenment are part of this movement. No individual will be able to claim all the glory for this achievement. It will be a group accomplishment that will be savored by all."

It was too bad Jesus couldn't come back to Earth one more time to lead us to enlightenment, I thought as I listened to Albert, although the Council no doubt had a different master plan for humans. Our discussion about Jesus and his miracles reminded me of an earlier conversation I had with Albert about Jesus and the scriptures that depicted his life and death. Albert had hinted that I would be astounded if I knew the real truth about Jesus, although he had declined to go any further at that time. Now I wanted to revisit this topic with Albert to see if he would be willing to share the startling truth about Jesus.

Chapter 11

The Secret Life of Jesus

When I was writing the manuscript for *Dancing on a Stamp*, Albert told me the soul that had incarnated as Jesus Christ was a very advanced soul, a Master, and that Jesus came to Earth to help humankind take the next step up the ladder of spiritual enlightenment. The fact that there are now over two billion Christians in the world clearly demonstrates that Jesus has had a very significant effect on human civilization. But one thing Albert mentioned in our conversations intrigued me and left me thirsting for more information. Albert had revealed that the gospels that described the life and death of Jesus had been edited and revised several times by the leaders of the Church after the original scriptures had been penned. This was done to ensure that the Holy Scriptures conformed to their vision of the Church and its beliefs.

Albert had not disclosed any details about what things were added or removed from the original gospels despite several attempts to glean this information from him. He usually responded that this information was not something I needed to know at the time; however, our recent discussion about Masters living on Earth spurred me to try one more time to pry some answers from Albert. So I steeled myself for my next question to him.

"You mentioned a while back, Albert, that the gospels about Jesus had been revised several times during the early days of the Church. I would dearly love to find out more about what was added or deleted from the scriptures, so I can learn the truth about this great man."

To my surprise, Albert was amenable to my request. "I can take you back to the Akashic Records so you view certain segments of the life of Jesus, but you should be careful what you ask for. Some of the things I will show you will be very controversial, and you may be ridiculed and subjected to hate and anger if you disclose these details in your book. Are you sure you want to do this?"

"You know what they say, the Lord hates a coward. Show me the truth about Jesus, and I will take my chances with the fallout."

Albert gave me one of his toothy smiles and nodded his head, like he already knew what my answer would be. He motioned for me to follow him, and he led me back to the Spirit Side and into the Hall of Records. We entered one of the vacant rooms and sat down beside the holographic globe in the center. Albert waved his hand over the globe, and the blue and white swirls gave way to a scene that I did not immediately recognize.

Albert explained that this scene was from the life of Jesus when he was seventeen years old. It was the day of the celebration feast for his marriage to Mary Magdalene. The globe displayed a large open square in the town of Nazareth, filled with long tables and wooden chairs. Several dozen jovial and animated guests were seated at the tables enjoying the sumptuous banquet and delicious red wine. The head table at the front of the square was adorned with an elaborate lace tablecloth and vases filled with fresh-cut flowers. I could see Jesus seated near the center of the head table, dressed in a simple white cotton tunic. He had shoulder-length hair and a neatly trimmed beard. Sitting to the left of Jesus were two of his younger brothers, James and Joseph. To the right of Jesus was his new bride, Mary Magdalene, with dazzling blue eyes and a radiant smile that reflected her jubilation. She was resplendent in a long white tunic made of fine silk and adorned with intricate needlework. Seated next to her were her bridesmaids, wearing understated linen tunics.

Albert advised that this was the wedding celebration feast for the marriage of Jesus and Mary Magdalene, which was the third part of a Jewish wedding during the time of Christ. The first two parts, the betrothal and the consummation, had already happened.

I could see that all the guests were having a wonderful time feasting on the wholesome food piled high on the platters and quaffing the ruby-red wine. Laughter and animated conversation filled the square with a joyful ambience. Jesus and Mary Magdalene glowed with happiness as they spent much time looking deeply into each other's eyes—almost oblivious to the festivities around them. I was fascinated by this scene as I sensed the strong bond of love between Jesus and Mary Magdalene.

So then I had to ask Albert the obvious question: "Are you telling me that Jesus Christ was married to Mary Magdalene, even though no mention of this is found in the scriptures?"

Albert shrugged his shoulders and smiled. "This marriage did happen because the Akashic Records do not lie. Several of the original gospels mentioned the marriage of Jesus; however, the subsequent edits by the Church leaders deleted all such references."

"Why were these edits made? What could be wrong with Jesus being married? Marriage was very common for Jewish men in the time of Christ, so why did they think Jesus should have remained single all of his life?"

"They did it for two reasons," Albert explained. "The first had to do with their characterization of Jesus as the son of God, part of the Holy Trinity. They felt that the son of God was a very special person who should not have been sullied by marriage to an ordinary human. They believed Jesus should not have had the usual attributes of mortal humans, including carnal desires, and Jesus would be held in higher esteem if he were celibate all of his life, thereby avoiding the impurities associated with sexual intercourse.

"The second reason was to avoid the distraction of his direct descendants laying claim to privileged positions in the Church because of their heritage. The holy men who revised the gospels, and who were not direct descendants of Christ, did not want their positions of power usurped by people who had a more direct connection to Jesus."

"Are you saying that Jesus had children?" I blurted out.

"Yes, of course, he did. Jesus and Mary Magdalene had two sons and one daughter. There is no mention of them in the scriptures because they were deleted as part of the editing process. They were not present during Christ's crucifixion and death, as they had been hidden by their mother with relatives for protection. Following Christ's death, Mary Magdalene and Mary, the mother of Jesus, concealed their identity and smuggled them out of Palestine to another country, where they lived normal lives, got married, and raised their own children. Their true identities were never discovered."

"Where did they live? Can you tell me who their descendants are?"

"I am not permitted to disclose this information at this time. This is something you do not need to know right now. It would serve no useful purpose. It would ignite a debate that would be divisive and distracting to all Christians. Humans need to focus on the present and not quarrel over the events of the past."

"So the Catholic Church's rationale for celibacy—that priests should be celibate because Jesus was celibate—has no real validity," I ventured.

"You are right. The Church's mandate for celibacy has been applied inconsistently over the centuries, and their current position has caused a lot of problems. Many of the priests who have been convicted for the sexual abuse of young children did so because they had no normal outlet for their sexual drive. If these priests had been allowed to marry, they would not have needed to fulfill their sexual cravings in abnormal and abusive ways. The Vatican still clings to this policy despite the recent rash of sexual assault convictions. Quite often, the first reaction of the Church leaders to allegations of sexual abuse by priests was to cover up these incidents and keep them out of the public eye. This doesn't work anymore, and they need to change their rule to prevent further abuse. They know this to be true, but, like most other older men on your planet, they are resistant to change.

"Although they cite Christ's celibacy as the reason for the rule, the real reason is an economic one. Priests with wives and children require more money to live than do single priests, and providing them with more remuneration would mean less money for the Church leaders to spend as they saw fit. Furthermore, if a priest should meet an untimely death, the Church would be obligated by public pressure to provide for the surviving wife and children, which would be another drain on the Church coffers. So it is unlikely they will change their position on celibacy any time soon, despite the obvious need to do so."

This was a lot of new information to digest, but the wedding scene raised another question in my mind: "Tell me about the two men seated next to Jesus, his younger brothers. As you know, the Catholic Church denies that Jesus had siblings. In fact, one of the mainstays of their beliefs is that his mother, Mary, was a virgin all of her life, something that would be untrue if she had other children after Jesus."

"Mary had four more sons and two daughters after Jesus," Albert continued, "and she conceived them in the normal fashion by having sexual intercourse with her husband. There are several references to the siblings of Jesus in the New Testament (which were missed when the other references were deleted), except the Church takes the position that these passages actually refer to cousins of Jesus or to the children of Joseph from a previous marriage, even though there is no evidence to support this view."

"Why did the Church think it necessary to deny this fact? What could be wrong with Mary having other children with her husband?"

"The early leaders of the Church felt that Mary should be venerated as a special person," Albert explained. "According to them, she was the mother of God and should be described in the best possible light. They believed she should be as pure as the driven snow, free of all human vices. In their distorted view of religious purity, this meant that Mary had to be depicted as a virgin all of her life, without any other children. This view stemmed from their underlying belief that sexual intercourse was a base and demeaning act that renders a person unholy and impure. The Church has continued to emphasize Mary's perpetual virginity to this very day. They often describe Mary as the 'blessed *virgin* Mary, mother of God.' It is interesting to note their emphasis on the word 'virgin,' like it was a badge of honor and something special to be proud of.

"In a way, though, it can be seen as demeaning to all the women throughout history who bore children the natural way—following intercourse with their husbands. Some people might even consider it a backhanded slam at all the loving and caring mothers who have been disparaged by the Church because they lost their virginity. It is the same misguided reasoning they used when they took their position that Jesus was celibate all of his life."

"This makes no sense to me," I responded. "Jesus and his mother were both humans, and it would be natural for them to marry and have sex, much like eating, drinking, and breathing are natural and essential activities of humans."

"I totally agree with you on this point. The Source created humans with sex organs and a strong sex drive by design, not by accident. There is nothing impure or unholy about sexual intercourse. The Church got off track about sex in the early days, led by men like Saint Augustine, and they still espouse this unnatural belief that sex (except by lawfully married couples for the purpose of conceiving a child) is sinful."

"So will these new revelations about Jesus, Mary Magdalene, and his mother, Mary, ever come to light?"

"There are documents in existence, although not yet publicly available, that disclose the truth about these matters. Some day they will be revealed, but this will not change the Church's position as it will deny their authenticity and claim them to be forgeries. In fact, if Jesus himself came down from Heaven and spoke the truth as he hovered over Saint Peter's square, the Vatican would claim it was just special effects developed in Hollywood."

"Am I allowed to mention this new information in my book?"

"Sure, go ahead. Many commentators have already asserted that Jesus had a wife and children, so one more voice would not add much to the cacophony. But be prepared for the hate and ridicule you may attract if you do so. If this happens, you can always blame it on the homeless man you met on the street one day. I have broad shoulders—and they won't be able to find me anyway."

As we left the Hall of Records, my head was spinning with this new information. Without a doubt, I knew I had to disclose these revelations in my book and take my chances. I was fortunate to be living in the twenty-first century when I wouldn't be burned at the stake for my sacrilege, although my chances of being invited for dinner with the Pope would be diminished considerably.

As I had a lot to absorb from this trip, I asked Albert to take me home. So he whisked me away from the Spirit Side and back to my bedroom, promising to return shortly with a few more bombshells.

Chapter 12

Planning with a Purpose

Although I loved pleasant surprises, the opposite kind could be distressing. And with Albert I never knew what to expect. I sometimes suspected he enjoyed keeping me off balance as a way of reminding me that I still had to finish my life on this planet, and my recent astral jaunts were merely a brief interlude from this difficult school. So while I waited for Albert to return so I could briefly escape the clutches of my purblind odyssey on Earth, I wondered once more why I had chosen to come here in the first place.

Surely there had to be places in the Universe where there were no taxes, no telemarketers, and no farcical sitcoms on television. Why didn't I choose a planet where I could eat as many cheeseburgers as I liked without breaking my scale and sending my cholesterol into the stratosphere? Or what about a nice tropical planet where I could spend my day on a white-sand beach sipping margaritas and munching on roast suckling pig, with my own personal manservant to help me squeeze into my XXL speedos every morning.

The answer was obvious to Albert, but not so much for me. Albert told me many times that I chose to come to this planet all on my own, and I should stop whining about it. And not only did I choose a journey on Earth, I had actually planned my life beforehand.

As I disclosed in *Dancing on a Stamp*, Albert revealed that we all create Life Plans before we incarnate. Our Life Plans establish the broad outlines of our lives on Earth that we design for the purpose of experiencing the things and learning the lessons we need for our evolution. We choose the significant details and events for our new incarnations, including our names and places of birth, the schools we will attend, and the people who will be our parents, siblings, spouses, children, and friends.

Albert had also explained that our Life Plans do not determine everything that happens in our lives. Because we have free will to take actions and make decisions while on Earth, and since we do not remember where we came from or what is in our Life Plans, we will often choose the wrong path when we come to a fork in the road.

While I understood my goal on Earth was to follow my Life Plan as best I could, I was curious about how I had developed my Life Plan on the Spirit Side. So the next time Albert appeared in my bedroom, I eagerly followed him up through the clouds to our usual perch high above Earth. And before Albert had a chance to speak, I blurted out my thoughts: "I am not sure what you had planned for tonight, Albert, but I have a request. I would like to observe a Life Planning session on the Spirit Side so I can better understand the process."

Albert nodded his agreement and led me to a stately edifice in Aglaia called the Hall of Planning. We entered through the large front door and strolled down a long hallway into a brightly lit room with a horseshoe table facing a large monitor on the wall. Seated around the table were twenty or so souls all dressed differently in colorful garments, much like the people I had seen on the streets of the city.

"This is a planning session for this group of souls who intend to incarnate as humans somewhere in North America. They plan to be born at various times during the next thirty years. I will let you listen to their deliberations, and then I will answer your questions," Albert revealed.

The soul seated at the center of the table, whose name was Elizabeth, led the discussion. She told the group that she had lived her last three lives on Earth as a male and felt it was time for her to experience her next life as a female. Elizabeth advised the group that she had assembled them to help plan her next incarnation because she wanted them to play major roles in her new life. In her two most recent lives she had been privileged and wealthy, with many servants to cater to her every wish. In one case, she had been the son of an earl in nineteenth-century Britain, and in her most recent life she had been a dashing Hollywood actor who had starred in several dozen successful movies. She had learned a lot about living in luxury without any worries about money, but admitted she had paid little attention to the plight of poor people in those lives. So now she wanted to experience a life of poverty.

Her plan for her next life was to be born to a poor family that had to struggle to pay the rent and put food on the table. She said she was targeting a small town in the Midwest of the United States and had chosen a newly married couple as her parents. The father, who was in his late twenties, was a bicycle messenger for a delivery company, while his younger wife waited tables at a local diner. They lived in a small apartment in a run-down building close to the diner. Despite their precarious financial circumstances, they wanted to have a baby.

Elizabeth pointed to the two souls sitting immediately to her left. She explained that these were the souls who had incarnated as the man and woman she had just described, and they had joined the meeting at her request so they could concur with her plan to incarnate as their first-born child.

(Albert had explained to me previously that all souls incarnated on Earth will temporarily leave their physical bodies every night during sleep to travel to the Spirit Side, although we are usually not allowed to remember these excursions. In this case, the souls of the prospective parents had joined the planning meeting during one of their nightly escapes.)

I listened with interest as the three of them discussed the pros and cons of this plan and the things each of them hoped to experience. When the arrangement had been agreed to in principle, they began to fill in the details: the name for the baby, and the souls who would be her siblings, childhood friends, and future husband. All of these souls, along with everyone else who would play a significant role in her life, were seated around the table, and the discussion was lively, but amicable. Despite all the different interactions her new life would involve, the group managed to reach an agreement on all matters. The outline of her new life was displayed on the wall monitor for all to see.

At this time Elizabeth pointed to three souls seated at the far right of the table who had not yet been assigned a role in her new life. She announced that she wanted them to be her spirit guides for the first part of her life because they had lived with poverty in a number of their previous lives on Earth and their guidance would be most helpful to her. The merits of her proposal were discussed at length until a consensus was reached that these three souls would serve as her guides.

The final step was approval by the Wise Ones. Two of the Council members entered the room and quickly scanned the monitor. They suggested a few changes to her Life Plan before giving Elizabeth their blessing.

Elizabeth's Life Plan was now final and ready for implementation. Everyone in the room dispersed, and Elizabeth left to bid farewell to others in her soul group before proceeding to the birthing room where she would be prepared for entry into the new baby at the appropriate time.

"This was a fascinating process," I commented to Albert. "Did I go through this before I was born?"

"Of course. Every soul has a similar life-planning process before it incarnates, and you were no exception. But as I mentioned before, your initial Life Plan is not etched in stone. You modify your Life Plan from time to time after your birth with changes you feel are necessary based on the things you have already experienced. You do this after consulting with your guides during one of your nightly journeys to the Spirit Side. The entire process is designed to be fluid and flexible so you can gain the most from your life on Earth.

"You can even change the exit points in your Life Plan so your soul can choose the best time for your physical body to die. This decision will be made by your soul based upon the experiences it has encountered and the lessons it has learned (or not learned)."

"It seems like a well-organized system," I agreed. "The only thing missing is being able to remember what is in my Life Plan when I am back in my human body. That would make my life so much easier."

"Your Life Plan amnesia is an important part of the whole scheme. If you knew what was in your Life Plan your life on Earth would be too easy. It would be like your teacher giving you the questions and answers to a final exam before the test. Trying to figure out what you had planned for yourself is one of the major challenges you face on Earth. It is the reason Earth is one of the toughest schools in the Universe. All humans should give themselves a big pat on the back because it took a lot of courage to incarnate on your harsh and difficult planet."

Although I knew Albert was right, I was still frustrated at my inability to remember the details of my Life Plan.

In the years before I met Albert, I had been searching for answers to all the "big questions" in life: Who am I? Why am I here? What am I supposed to accomplish during my life? And where do I go after I die? When I recalled my earlier conversations with Albert, I had to acknowledge that he gave me good answers to most of my questions, which I recited in *Dancing on a Stamp*.

Even though I took great comfort from Albert's revelations, his response to my question about what I was supposed to accomplish in my life left me only partially satisfied. I understood I was supposed to live my life in accordance with the Life Plan I had created before I was born, even though I was not allowed to remember what was in this blueprint for my life. And the more I thought about it, the more dissatisfied I became with his answer. While it was comforting to know there was a plan for my life, one I had created, I still did not know any specifics about my purpose for being here. As it stood now, I could only guess about my life purpose, and I would never know if I was on track or way off course until after I died.

Albert's justification for the blindfolds we are forced to wear on Earth made sense, although I wondered if there was a middle ground on this issue. Was there a way for us to determine the general direction we should be heading without learning all the specifics?

Albert told me I should not be concerned about the details of my Life Plan because no matter how far I strayed off course I would always return to the Spirit Side when my life on Earth was over. And anything I missed in this life could be experienced in another life, since I could incarnate over and over until I had encountered everything on Earth I needed for my evolution.

But this knowledge did not help me that much in this life. Even though I was an eternal soul with no deadlines or timetables for my evolution, I did not relish the prospect that I might have to live hundreds more lives on this planet, floundering around blindly until I managed somehow to experience all the things on my checklist. There had to be a better way to handle this quandary.

Albert's response on this point reminded me of the infinite monkey theorem I had debated with my college roommates long ago: if you have a monkey sitting at a keyboard and randomly striking the keys for an infinite amount of time, will it eventually type out the complete Bible, word for word? The answer to this philosophical enigma is not important, even though its resemblance to the potential randomness of my life on Earth was somewhat unsettling.

I did not savor the thought of taking forever to graduate from this planet so I could move on to the next stage of my evolution. I was eager to explore the vast Universe and the millions of planets with life forms, and I did not want to linger on Earth any longer than necessary. The Universe was beckoning, and I did not want to keep it waiting.

I had a feeling Albert had been holding something back when he had responded to my query about my life purpose—and I decided to revisit this topic.

"Can you tell me, Albert, how I can find out more about my life purpose? How can I discover the general direction I should be heading?"

Albert yielded to my persistence and responded: "There are ways for you to see glimpses of your Life Plan and your purpose in this life, although you will never be allowed to see all the details. Let me outline a few simple steps that will provide you with some guidance."

"To begin, you must understand that you do not have only one principal life purpose—you have had a different life purpose for each stage of your life so far. When you were a young child, your life purpose was to explore your environment, learn new things, and have fun. Once you started school, your life purpose was to focus on completing your formal education and learning how to interact with others in your society.

"When you completed your formal education, your life purpose was to choose a career that made you happy and fulfilled, marry the woman of your dreams, and raise your children. And when you retired from the law, your life purpose changed once again.

"The most difficult part for everyone is choosing a career because there are so many choices. So how do you know if the career you choose is right for you? If you are eager to go to work most days, and you generally enjoy your job, you are on the right track. (Keep in mind that no one will enjoy his or her work 100 percent of the time.) You have the right job if you can become totally engrossed with your work every now and then without being aware of the passage of time. But, if you have to drag yourself into work every day you likely should be looking for a new job. Your feelings about your career are affected by the messages you receive every day from your soul and spirit guides. If you are off track and haven't found your life purpose for any stage of your life, these messages will reinforce your feeling that your life is unbalanced in some way. You should heed this subtle advice and make the changes you need to get back on track.

"Once you understand changes are needed, the more difficult task is to find out what you should be doing next. Most often your guidance will arise from external events you will notice in your life—especially coincidental events. You must be vigilant to recognize these signs and understand what they mean. For example, you might notice a new billboard on your way to work that attracts your attention, one that touts the virtues of a company you have never heard of before. If you find there is something compelling about this billboard, and you continue to think about it throughout your day, it may be a sign that you should seek a job with this company.

"If you happen to get a phone call out of the blue from a former classmate you haven't spoken to in years, pay special attention to what this person says; her words may contain a hidden clue to steer you in the right direction. Your guides will send you messages through many different channels, and you must be alert to recognize them for what they are.

"If you are frustrated at not being able to discover your life purpose for any stage of your life, you should practice meditation on a regular basis. This will help to calm your mind and allow you to become better at hearing the messages and recognizing the signs being sent your way.

"Unfortunately, there is no easy way to determine your life purpose once you become an adult. It is a challenge for all humans—yet one that can be overcome with concerted effort and patience. As I have told you often before, this is why life on Earth is no walk in the park."

We left the Hall of Planning and Albert guided me down into my bedroom once again, where I slid back into my body. The next morning I remembered my visit to the Hall of Planning in vivid detail, which helped me understand the pre-birth planning process, although I was still not any wiser about the details of my own Life Plan. I resolved to ask Albert to take me back to the Hall of Records so I could view some of my past lives, with the expectation that this would shed light on what I needed to experience in this life. I truly hoped that the good things I had done in my previous lives would outweigh the bad.

Chapter 13

Past Lives Remembered

I was ready for Albert when he returned for our next astral trek. As soon as we reached our customary assembly spot, I tugged gently at his sleeve and made my pitch: "Before you take me anywhere, I have a request. Can we go back to the Hall of Records? I would like to review a few of my past lives to see if this will help me better understand my purpose in this life."

Albert shrugged his shoulders and responded, "You know I cannot reveal your Life Plan for this life, but I can show you several of your past lives as long as you let me choose the ones that will help you understand the challenges in your current life."

"Fine with me, Albert, lead the way."

I followed Albert through the doorway into the Spirit Side and then into the Hall of Records, where Albert announced his plan. "I am going to show you a life you had in Ancient Greece. You were a scholar who studied astronomy, and you were recognized throughout Athens as an expert in your field, although many citizens believed your teachings were too radical. I will show you a scene when you were thirty-four and tutoring a young man named Demas."

When the scene in the holographic globe came into focus, I could see myself as man in his physical prime—tall and slim, with jet-black hair touching my shoulders and a neatly trimmed beard. I was wearing a short white tunic tied at the waist with a black sash, with sandals on my feet. Demas, who was in his late teens, sat cross-legged on a small bench, listening attentively to my lecture.

I listened to my speech with great fascination. "Today, Demas, I will teach you about our planet and its closest neighbors—as recorded by the Ancient Seers who acquired this knowledge centuries ago from an alien race who traveled here from the Orion constellation. These records have been secretly passed down from scholar to scholar over the centuries, and I now have the responsibility to keep them safe until I pass them on to you.

"Contrary to current thinking, the records from the Ancient Seers disclose that Earth is not the center of the universe. Earth revolves around our sun, which is a small star near the outer edge of a galaxy containing billions of stars. Our sun has nine planets in its system, with Earth being the third innermost planet. None of the other planets has life as we know it on Earth, although Mars did sustain life eons ago.

"According to the Ancient Seers, millions of years ago Mars had oceans and rivers and an atmosphere similar to our planet today. It had many different life forms and plants, some of which were like those found on Earth today. It was also the first home for humans in our solar system. A race of extraterrestrials (ETs) from Orion seeded human life on Mars long before humans arrived on Earth. Mars was chosen as the first birthing ground for humans because of its favorable climate and atmosphere. At that time, Earth was still in its formative stages with hundreds of active volcanoes and a toxic atmosphere.

"Human civilization on Mars began at a primitive stage, with humans sustaining themselves as hunter-gatherers. With a lot of help from the ETs, however, they rapidly progressed into the technological era— much faster than humans did on Earth. It was an experiment to see if humans could handle rapid technological advances without tragic consequences. The ETs helped humans build large structures with their antigravity devices, showed them how to harness the power of crystals, and taught them how to heal injuries and prevent disease.

"Unfortunately, the ETs failed miserably when it came to human emotions. Humans had become a lot more intelligent and knowledgeable with the help of the ETs, except they had not progressed as much with emotional intelligence. All the negative emotions, like fear, hate, anger, and greed, were still very prevalent with the humans, and this led to disastrous consequences.

"With their advanced technology they began to investigate the asteroids that orbited the sun between Mars and Jupiter. They learned that many asteroids were rich with the minerals Mars needed to sustain its civilization. So a few of their scientists came up with a plan to develop a very powerful tractor beam that could be used to drag one of the asteroids into an orbit around Mars where it could be mined easily. But other groups were opposed to this plan because they feared this technology was not refined enough to ensure the asteroid would not spin out of control and smash into their planet, and they did not want to take the risk.

"The proponents of this scheme were determined to proceed as they were confident their plan would be successful without any disastrous consequences. Their opponents were equally determined to stop this plan, and a bitter conflict ensued. Ultimately, the proponent group tried to use this powerful energy beam to quell the rebellion, except they did not fully understand the energy they were dealing with. They ended up unleashing forces they could not control, and all life on Mars perished with the total destruction of their civilization, rendering the planet the lifeless wasteland it is today.

"The ETs could see what was developing, although they were not permitted to stop it. Instead, they scooped up some of the humans before the destruction and sustained them on another planet until conditions on Earth were more hospitable. Then they began all over by seeding our planet with the human survivors from Mars. Only this time they realized that rapid technological advances without corresponding advances in emotional intelligence were a recipe for disaster. So they let humans on Earth develop slowly at their own pace without any quantum leaps in technology.

"Today on our planet we have progressed from our primitive days, but our handling of negative emotions, especially greed and the desire for power, is still lacking. Fortunately, we have not yet developed the technology to destroy all life on Earth. We must work hard to rid ourselves of the negative emotions that are holding us back as a race. We need to learn the lessons from our past on Mars."

Demas sat there quietly, enthralled by my discourse. Then, without any warning, a group of young men burst into the room, brandishing swords. They shouted "death for the sorcerer" and stabbed us repeatedly until our bodies lay limply in a pool of blood. *So much for controlling negative emotions*, I thought.

"Why did these men kill us?" I asked Albert.

"They thought your teachings were dangerous and blasphemous, and they feared wrath from the gods if they didn't stop the sacrilege. And because your views were so radical, they believed you were in league with the devil. They were propelled by fear and superstition to take matters into their own hands.

"Killings like this have been a common occurrence in the history of humankind on Earth. The victims were often people who were eccentric and didn't fit into the norm. And many others were persecuted because of the color of their skin or the religion they followed. Humans have always had a tendency to fear what they don't understand and the people who look or act differently."

I shuddered and turned away until Albert waved his hand over the sphere and this scene disappeared. Although I did not relish the thought of watching any more tragic lives, my curiosity was aroused, and I turned back to the holographic globe as Albert conjured up a new image.

This time I was a man in my early thirties in England in the eighteenth century. I was a shoemaker with a small shop on a side street in Manchester. I lived with my wife and two young children, aged two and five, in a small flat above the shop. Business had been slow for the last few months, and we had run out of money. I had not eaten in several days so my wife and children could finish the last of our food. And with winter just around the corner, we desperately needed more coal to burn in our small stove.

So I put on my ragged jacket and left the shop, walking toward the large, fancy houses near the center of town. I trudged down the back alley behind a row of these mansions, hoping to find food that had been discarded by the servants. I noticed a bucket sitting beside the back door of a large brick house, and I quietly snuck closer to get a better look. It was full of apples that were bruised and partially rotten, obviously unfit for the family of the house. I assumed these apples were going to be picked up by one of the local farmers and fed to the hogs.

I looked around to see if anyone was watching, but the coast was clear. So I quickly reached into the bucket to grab six of the apples, which I tucked into my coat pocket. I turned to make my escape, but it was too late. A strong hand clasped my shoulder and spun me around. Before I could break free, a large man wearing a white apron wrestled me to the ground, shouting for help. Soon two more kitchen workers rushed out the door and tied my hands behind my back. The large man sent one of the others into the street to find a constable. The copper arrived shortly and, after hearing that I had tried to steal apples from the kitchen, he hauled me off to the station and threw me in a jail cell.

I was locked up for several days, subsisting on stale crusts of bread and slimy water, without any way of contacting my wife. Then one day they led me from the cell into a courtroom presided over by a magistrate. The constable who arrested me explained to the court that I had been caught in the act of stealing apples from a private residence. Despite my plea that the half-rotten apples had been left outside the kitchen as food for the hogs, and that I had taken them to feed my starving family, the magistrate convicted me of theft and sentenced me to death by hanging.

One week later, I was hauled out of my cell and marched up to the gallows that stood beside the jail. It was hanging day, and the square was filled with onlookers who had come to see the spectacle. With my hands tied behind my back, I was positioned over the trap door with a noose around my neck and a black hood over my head. Then I heard the creak of a lever, and the floor disappeared beneath me. I hung there for a split second until gravity won the day, and I dropped until I reached the end of the rope …

I had to look away from this scene, which I found frightening and disgusting, even though I knew my soul had survived the hanging.

"How could a so-called civilized society let this happen?" I asked Albert. "Those apples were of no use to those people, although they could have provided much-needed nourishment for my starving family. How could they have been so callous? What kind of justice system imposes the death penalty for petty theft? And what happened to my wife and children after that?"

"They had to resort to begging for food in the street, since you were the only one who could make shoes to generate income. That winter during a bad cold spell they froze to death, huddled together under a few thin blankets, because they had no wood or coal to fuel their stove," Albert explained.

"So the gross injustice they served on me resulted in suffering and death for my family, who were innocent of any wrongdoing. This was utterly disgusting and shameful."

Albert nodded his agreement, and responded: "In those days privileged people were often self-centered with little regard for poor people. They did not feel any compassion for their fellow humans and almost never forgave anyone for their misdeeds, however minor they might be. What happened to you in that life was fairly typical for that society, as unthinkable as it may seem to you now. The good news is that humans have made a lot of progress in the last few centuries in dealing with disadvantaged people, although there are still societies in your world that have not advanced much since these dark days you just witnessed."

"As an aside, Albert, before I met you I often wondered if I had been hung from the gallows in one of my previous lives. I have a dark patch of skin on the front of my neck, like a birthmark, and I have always hated tight collars on my shirts. Now I think I know why—it stems from that awful day long ago when I died at the end of a noose."

"You are likely right about that since residual memories of previous lives sometimes leak through to later lives, often in the form of physical anomalies," Albert concurred. "You should know, however, that this was not the only time you died from a constricted windpipe. Once you were strangled by your wife to stop your loud, incessant snoring, and in another life you were throttled by the tribal chief to ensure that none of your stupid genes could be passed down to the next generation. It is no wonder you are sensitive about your neck!"

"Why don't we just continue with my past lives, Albert? I am not in the mood for your macabre humor."

"All right then," Albert conceded with an impish grin. "Let me show you a scene from another eventful life that taught you a very valuable lesson."

I focused once more on the globe as the blue and white swirls gave way to a new scene showing Wyoming in the 1870s. In this life I was a gambler who drifted from town to town playing poker in the local saloons. And when I wasn't gambling, I practiced drawing and shooting my six-shooter over and over until I became faster and more accurate than most other men—a talent that had served me well on many occasions.

The scene in the globe crystallized on a small frontier town in the old West. I rode my horse into town, tied it up at the hitching post, and walked through the double swinging doors into the saloon. I scanned the room as I sipped on a beer, looking for a poker game to join. I noticed one table with a lot of cash in the player stashes and an empty chair. I sauntered over to this table and asked to join the game. They quickly agreed when I flashed a large roll of bills from my pocket. I was dealt in on the next hand, and within a couple of hours I had cleaned out all but one of the players. He was a fat little man who looked like a merchant. He had been drinking heavily all afternoon, which did not help with his game. On the last hand, he went all-in and I called. He flashed a big grin as he showed me his hand—kings over eights, but his smile turned into a scowl when I laid down my three queens.

He immediately jumped to his feet and accused me of cheating. I did not respond as I scooped up my winnings and walked toward the door. The chubby little man became enraged, shouting once more that I was a cheater as he challenged me to a gunfight in the street. I knew I could easily outdraw this foolish man, and I did not want to kill him, so I continued out the door to get on my horse. The little man followed me out of the saloon, shouting loudly that I was a cheater and a coward. A small crowd had gathered nearby to listen to the exchange. I tried my best to ignore the taunts, but his shrill insults were irritating and very hurtful to my pride. No one likes to be called a cheater and a coward in front of a crowd of people, especially since I had never before backed away from a challenge.

And so the dark side won the day as I ignored the little whisper in my head that pleaded with me to ride out of town. I turned to the furious little man and accepted his challenge. We both walked to the center of the street and stood there facing each other, poised for action.

After a few seconds, my opponent, who was sweating profusely, reached for his gun. I quickly drew mine and dropped him with one clean shot to his chest. He had not even been able to get his gun completely out of its holster. I got on my horse and slowly rode out of town. I didn't feel elated or proud of myself, and I decided then and there that my gambling days were over. I knew the fat little man had not deserved to die that way, and I resolved to swallow my pride in the future.

So I turned my horse around and rode back into town. I could see the dead man's widow hugging his head to her bosom and weeping quietly. She looked at me with fearful eyes as I approached. I told her I was sorry for killing her husband and handed her all the cash I had won at the poker table. I rode back out of town feeling good about my gift to the widow, even though nothing would ever make up for my sin of pride that had cost this man his life.

"I feel awful about that incident, Albert. I am ashamed about all the suffering I caused because of my wounded pride."

"This was one of the important lessons you learned in your journeys on Earth. In order to fully appreciate this experience, you planned your next life as someone who would be on the receiving end of violence arising from a perceived breach of honor."

The globe now displayed a new scene in India early in the twentieth century. In this life, I was a pretty girl in her mid-teens, with long dark hair, light brown skin, and large hazel eyes. On this day I wore a turquoise silk sari with gold slippers on my feet, and I was sitting in a large room furnished with brocade sofas and chairs, elegant teak tables, and an intricate wool rug on the floor. Seated opposite me were my grim-faced parents who were determined to win an argument with their daughter, which became louder and more animated with each passing minute.

Albert explained that my parents, who were wealthy merchants, had followed the custom of their society by arranging my marriage to a young man from another affluent family who were held in high regard. My parents had just revealed this plan to me, and I was very upset. I was a rebellious spirit, and I thought that the custom of arranged marriages was outdated and abusive. I believed I should be able to freely choose my husband—someone I could love for the rest of my life. I told my parents I would not marry the young man they had chosen for me because I had never met him and certainly did not love him. The argument went on for several hours, and even the tears streaming down my face would not deter my parents. They said they had given their word to the other family, and it would be a terrible dishonor to our family if the marriage did not proceed as planned.

Realizing the futility of my position, I ran from the room and up the stairs to my bedroom, where I flung myself on the bed, sobbing uncontrollably. No one came to console me, not even my mother. Every day for the next few weeks I pleaded with my parents to stop the marriage and let me choose my own husband. But my entreaties fell on deaf ears, and they refused to change their plans.

As the day of the wedding approached, I became more and more desperate for a way to avoid having a stranger foisted into my life as my husband. I could see nothing ahead of me other than a miserable life of living with a man I did not love. *How could my parents be so pig-headed?* I wondered. *How could they ignore the wishes of their only daughter—someone they used to dote on like I was the most precious child in the world?*

It was obvious I had to do something or my worst nightmare would come true. So two days before the wedding, I snuck out of my house in the wee hours of the morning and ran down the street, not knowing where I was going or what I would do. I ended up in a boardinghouse several miles from my home, renting a small room with the cash I had stashed in my bedroom. I had only one bag stuffed with clothes and jewelry. I wore a dark, unadorned sari so I would not attract attention. The lady who ran the boardinghouse suspected I had run away from home, although she did not let on that she knew. She was happy to take my money and keep quiet until she could determine my true identity and collect any reward my family might have posted.

My parents were concerned the next morning when I did not come down for breakfast, and fearful when they found my room empty. But then they became enraged when they read the note I had left for them:

Dear Mother and Father,

I cannot go through with the marriage you have arranged for me. I have tried to dissuade you from proceeding with this plan over the last few weeks, but you have refused to change your minds. Regretfully, I now have no choice but to leave this house and make my own way in life, hopefully finding a kind and loving man I can wed—someone who will love and protect me as any husband should. I know in my heart there is such a man out there, and I will find him. I hope you will come to your senses at some point and welcome me back into your arms. Except for your insistence on my forced marriage, you have always been kind and loving parents, and I thank you for all you have done for me. I will always love you with all of my heart. Please forgive me for doing this, but I have no alternative.

Your loving daughter,

Riya

They immediately scoured the neighborhood and notified the police, but I was not to be found. The wedding had to be called off, much to the shame and embarrassment of my parents, the groom, and the groom's parents. My parents became the objects of gossip and ridicule by their peers, and every day my father became more enraged at my disobedience. He seethed at the unthinkable humiliation and dishonor he had to suffer because of my actions.

I was very careful in the weeks following to remain hidden in my room, venturing out only when necessary with my head mostly covered. Then one day the lady of the house learned about the disappearance of the daughter of a prominent merchant family, and she immediately connected the dots. She discretely contacted my father to claim the reward.

Shortly after, my solitude was shattered when my father burst into my room. He did not hug me like a loving father who has found his missing daughter. Instead, he approached me menacingly as I cowered in the corner, his face a mask of rage. Without speaking a word, he pulled a long knife from his sash and stabbed me over and over in my chest and belly. I screamed and slumped to the floor in a pool of blood, as the vision of my father hovering over me slowly dimmed and gave way to darkness.

As I watched this horrific scene, I could once again feel the anguish and betrayal I had felt in that life as my father stabbed me repeatedly. Then, much to my relief, Albert waved his hand over the globe and this scene disappeared.

"This was terrible, Albert. What could have possessed this man to kill his only daughter in cold blood?"

"In this society they had a very strong, but hopelessly misguided, sense of honor," Albert replied. "To this man, honor was more important than anything else. And your refusal to marry the man he had chosen for you was, in his distorted view, the ultimate act of dishonor, which unleashed his uncontrollable anger and hate. Your disobedience was so shameful and humiliating to him that his love for you was totally overwhelmed by his wounded pride. So he felt he had no choice except to you kill you in order to redeem his family's honor. This was a prime example of negative emotions trumping love and compassion.

"In your life as a gambler, you let your pride goad you into killing a bumbling fool. And when you suffered a tragic death in this life at the hands of your father, you were then able to truly understand the great harm that often results from false pride and false honor.

"Authentic pride, which is a feeling of accomplishment and satisfaction with your work, or with the achievements of your family, is a good thing. It spurs you to do your very best in all of your endeavors and to appreciate similar efforts by your friends, family, and coworkers. False pride, however, stems from vanity and insecurity. It can prod you to lash out at those people who do not hold you and your talents in the high esteem you feel is warranted. False pride can cause a lot of damage when you strive to prove your naysayers wrong in a negative fashion.

"Similarly, authentic honor is a self-imposed imperative that will motivate you to be honest, fair, and compassionate with everyone in order to earn their admiration and respect. False honor is an unwarranted expectation that your family must obey your wishes and adhere to the customs of your society, failing which you will be humiliated and shamed in the eyes of your peers. As you just witnessed from your life in India, false honor can tear families apart with the hate and anger it often generates.

"You must understand it is difficult to lose your negative emotions and actions if you pay too much attention to what others think of you. If you want to free yourself from the dark side, you must learn to ignore the negative comments coming from others because you are the one who truly understands the path you have chosen in this life."

Although I was still shaken by the scene in India, I understood why Albert had shown me that life with its tragic ending. I silently hoped Albert would show me a life with a happier result. With some reluctance, I focused once more on the globe as a new scene displaced the swirls.

This time I saw myself as a young man walking along a dirt road in the countryside. Albert explained that I was the son of a poor peasant farmer in sixteenth-century France who had been sent to the local village to buy a loaf of bread. Times were tough for my family, as the crop that year was substandard and we didn't know if we would have enough food to survive the winter.

I clutched the loaf tightly to my side, knowing this was all my mom, dad, and little sister would have to eat for dinner. My stomach growled from hunger as I plodded back toward our modest hovel. But before I reached my home, I came upon a crippled man sitting by the side of the road. His clothes were soiled and ragged and his hands were crusted with dirt. He called out to me as I approached: "Please, good sir, can you give me a piece of your bread. I have not eaten anything in days."

I looked into his watery brown eyes that were filled with fear and desperation. I hesitated briefly, torn between two thoughts. I felt sorry for this poor man, and I truly wanted to help him. But I also knew my hungry family could not spare any of the bread. And then I heard a whisper in my mind—a little voice that beseeched me to help this poor man. So I broke the loaf in half and gave him one of the pieces. His eyes shone with love and gratitude, and he flashed me a warm smile. He mumbled his thanks as he broke off small chunks and stuffed them in his mouth.

I continued my trek back home, now very afraid of what my parents would say when I arrived with only half a loaf. As soon as I walked through the door I blurted out my story about the crippled man—fully expecting to be chastised for my foolishness. Much to my surprise, they listened quietly until I was finished and then hugged me warmly. They told me I had done the right thing, and we would make do with only half a loaf. Although I went to bed hungry that night, I felt good about helping the crippled man and relieved that my parents were not angry with me.

Two days later, in the late afternoon, there was a knock at our door. It was the crippled man who had begged for half of our bread. He entered our shack and emptied his bag on our table. Out came four loaves of bread, along with heaps of potatoes, cabbages, and carrots and several rings of sausage. He grinned as he told us the food was ours to enjoy.

He explained that he had been in the village the day before, begging for food, when he had noticed a small child playing in the middle of the road. She was totally unaware of a horse-drawn wagon approaching at a fast clip, the driver unable to see her. Our benefactor hurried onto the road as best he could, scooped up the little girl, and whisked her out of harm's way in the nick of time. The little girl's father, who had witnessed the whole scene, thanked him with tear-filled eyes as he hugged his daughter tenderly. As a reward for this brave deed, the father gave him a bag full of food and hired him to help bake bread in his bakery. And because the crippled man knew he would now be able to feed himself in the future, he had decided to give all this food to us as repayment for our generosity.

We hugged him and waved good-bye as he hobbled back toward the village. I never saw this man again, and the baker told me he had disappeared shortly after saving his daughter. I sensed this crippled man was someone special who had appeared in that life to teach me about the magic of compassion and generosity, but Albert would not comment on his true identity.

This scene disappeared from the globe, and I thanked Albert for showing me this episode from that life. I felt good about what I had done and was humbled by the actions of the crippled man. I resolved to remember this lesson when I returned to my life on Earth.

Albert waved his hand over the globe once again and another new scene appeared. Albert explained that this was a life I had in Vienna in the seventeenth century. I was the daughter of a count and lived a life of pampered luxury in our opulent palace with my mother, father, and older brother. My father and mother were very wealthy as they both came from a long line of nobility in Austria.

I was fifteen and still single, with long dark hair and radiant green eyes. I loved to dress in long silk dresses and wear gold bangles encrusted with precious jewels. The scene focused on my bedroom, which was richly decorated with intricate wall hangings, elegant oak and walnut furniture, and a large four-poster bed. I was waking up from a night's sleep as one of my servants entered with a breakfast tray laden with fresh fruit and pastries, orange juice, and a pot of tea. As soon as the servant left, my lady-in-waiting, Anna, entered my bedroom and sat on a chair beside my bed. I could tell she had something on her mind, so I asked her to speak up about her concerns.

Anna told me that the day before she had caught Maria, one of the maids who looked after my bedroom, stealing a gold bracelet from my jewelry case. She said Maria had broken down, sobbing with fear and regret, as she explained she needed the bracelet to buy her sister's freedom from her life as a slave girl in North Africa. A few months before, her sister had been captured by Algerian pirates when she was traveling through Palestine with a group of merchants on a trading mission. The pirates had attacked the caravan at night, killing all the men and capturing the women as slaves. Her sister was eventually sold to a wealthy merchant from Egypt. Maria never found out what had happened to her sister, although she feared the worst.

Two days before, Maria had stumbled upon her sister in the merchant's entourage in one of Vienna's markets. Maria learned from the slave master that her sister could be purchased out of slavery for a large sum of money. And since the merchant and his retinue would be leaving Vienna within the next week to return home, she knew she had to act quickly if she hoped to save her sister.

Anna confided that she had not told anyone about this incident because she wanted to speak to me first. Anna feared that Maria would be severely punished if her crime was reported, and she did not wish that to happen because she was very fond of Maria. Tears welled up in Anna's eyes as she pleaded with me to conceal the crime from my father. She told me the bracelet had since been returned to my jewelry case and no harm had been done. Anna reminded me that Maria was really a good person who had acted out of desperation in order to save her sister from a life of slavery.

I really liked Maria, and I greatly admired and respected Anna. I knew my father would be furious if he found out, and he would see to it that Maria was punished to the fullest extent of the law.

I had an extensive collection of beautiful and expensive jewelry, and I never would have missed this gold bracelet if Maria had been able to pull off her caper. So I made a quick decision and asked Anna to fetch Maria. A grim-faced Anna returned several minutes later with Maria, who was sobbing with fear.

I used my lace handkerchief to dry her tears while giving her a reassuring smile. I looked into her wide eyes and told her everything was going to be all right, as I would not report her crime to my father so long as she promised to never steal again. Maria quickly made her promise to me and thanked me profusely for my generosity. Then I surprised her by handing Anna a sack full of gold coins to be used to buy Maria's sister from the slave master. Maria's smile could have lit up the darkest room on a cloudy day. She thanked me again, kissed my cheek, and sped out the door with Anna.

As I sat alone in my room, I was confident I had done the right thing, and I thanked God that He had given me the courage to make a positive difference in someone's life.

The scene in the globe slowly gave way to the blue and white swirls, and I turned to face Albert.

"Thank you, Albert, for showing me this life. I am thrilled that I was generous to the young servant girl, and I only wish I could have been as kind in all of my previous lives. I need time to reflect on what you have shown me today, and someday I would like to come back here to view more of my past lives."

I followed Albert out of the Hall of Records and back toward Earth. We drifted down to my house and back into my bedroom. I waved good-bye to Albert as I slipped back into my body. The next morning I awoke with a start, mulling over everything I had witnessed on my last visit to the Hall of Records. I felt happy and sad at the same time.

Even though the past could not be changed, I believed I could still shape my future. So I leapt out bed and resolved to do my best to make the world a better place. And I already knew what I wanted to ask Albert the next time he came calling—and my heart skipped a beat as I eagerly anticipated his return.

Chapter 14

Even the Bad Guys Go to Heaven

In the days following my visit to the Hall of Records to view my past lives, I had mixed feelings about this experience. I felt guilty about the harm I had inflicted on others in the past, even if it was not intentional, but I was elated about those lives where I had managed to do some good. I was most troubled by my life in India, and I wondered how my father in that life had been able to cope with his Life Review after his life on Earth had ended.

For that matter, I was still somewhat troubled by Albert's assertion in my first book that murderers and terrorists all returned to the Spirit Side when they died. Like most people, I was raised with strong views about what was right or wrong. I expected that people who breached the laws of the country would be punished for their misdeeds, which I believed to be fair and just. The Catholic Church had also taught me that anyone who committed a sin (and did not make amends before leaving this world) would be judged and punished by God. Given this background, the thought that a murderer would return to the Spirit Side after death seemed hard to swallow.

So on his very next visit, I decided to ask Albert to explain once more why bad people went to Heaven.

"Why do murderers return to the Spirit Side when they die?" I pressed him. "Why should the bad people end up in the same place as the good people? And if I know the Source will not punish me for bad behavior on Earth, why would I choose to be good?"

Albert looked at me like my mother often did when I asked why it was time for bed. "Let me begin by answering your second question first.

Although the Source does not make rules for humans to follow on Earth and does not punish them for anything they do, human societies have made their own laws to maintain peace and security for their citizens. Humans must obey these rules or they will be punished by their secular governments. So even if you believe there will be no punishment for your crimes in the afterlife, you will still need to follow the laws of the land to avoid punishment on Earth."

"Even if there were no secular laws in your country, most people would not commit serious crimes because it would be contrary to their innate sense of right and wrong, which stems from the messages they get from their guides and their higher self. If your government announced one day that they had repealed the crime against murder, most people would not go out and kill someone because intuitively they know it to be wrong. There would be exceptions to this pattern of conduct, however, just as there are exceptions on your planet today where murders are committed on a regular basis even though it is prohibited by secular laws.

"The view that murderers should suffer some form of punishment in the afterlife is understandable, but misguided. You are looking at things from an Earthly perspective and basing your beliefs on what you have been taught all of your life. Once you cross over to the Spirit Side your will understand what life on Earth is really all about and why criminals are not punished in the afterlife.

"In reality, your planet is like a grand theater and all humans are acting in a play. You scripted your role in this play when you prepared your Life Plan, and you continue to write and rewrite your part through your free-will actions on Earth.

"Imagine that you are acting in a play on Earth, and the script requires you to stab and kill another actor. When the curtain goes down and you leave the theater, you will not be arrested by the police for murder because it was just a play and the murder did not really happen. Likewise, when the soul of a murderer returns to the Spirit Side, it will not be punished for this deed since the souls on the Spirit Side understand that humans are acting in a grand play, and the crimes committed on Earth are part of this play. Nothing that happens on Earth is for keeps, and there are no lasting effects that carry over to the Spirit Side, other than the memories and wisdom gained from each incarnation. The soul of the murder victim will feel no hatred or anger toward the perpetrator, who will be forgiven without hesitation and embraced with unconditional love."

"Why do murders happen on Earth?" I inquired. "Are they all set out beforehand in our Life Plans?"

"Humans inflict injury or death on others for one of two reasons. Sometimes it was planned before incarnation and incorporated into the Life Plans of the souls involved. In these cases, either the soul to be murdered wanted to experience a violent death as part of its evolution, or the souls of the victim's loved ones wanted to learn how to cope with the brutal death of a family member as part of their life lessons. In order to fulfill these desires, they would have recruited another soul to play the part of the villain.

"In other situations, the murder was not planned before birth, and the crime was committed when the free-will actions of the perpetrator were unduly influenced by uncontrollable negative emotions. These occurrences are considered part of life on Earth, and the murderer is not denigrated because all souls know that negative emotions will often cause humans to stray off course. Souls that choose to incarnate on Earth fully expect to encounter harmful actions from time to time as a result of free-will actions running amok."

"So what happens in a murderer's Life Review?" I wondered.

"It is the same as all other Life Reviews. If the murder was a planned event, the soul of the perpetrator will understand it was merely following the script. If the murder was not planned, the soul will carefully analyze the events that led to this crime in order to better understand what caused it to veer so far off course. The soul of the murderer will not feel guilty or embarrassed because it will understand the true nature of life on Earth."

"You make it all sound so simple and carefree," I countered.

"That is because you are accustomed to treating everything that happens on Earth too seriously. If you flub your lines in a school play, you will likely laugh at your mistake when your part is over. You must try to think of life on Earth in a similar fashion. You need to lighten up and enjoy your journey since you cannot go wrong or become lost.

You will always return to the Spirit Side regardless of how well you played your part on Earth. And you can return to Earth as often as you like until you are satisfied with your performance."

It was difficult to argue with his logic, which was usually the case whenever I challenged Albert to explain why so many of the things I had been taught as a child were fallacious.

I still had a lot more questions for Albert on my checklist, and I was anxious to spring them on him before he disappeared into the sunset. I had learned several things about the past from my visits to the Hall of Records, and I wondered if it was possible for me to get a glimpse into my future. I hoped Albert would have an answer that would not disappoint.

Chapter 15

The Future Is Already Here

Like most humans, I have often contemplated the future and wondered what I would be doing next year or even five years down the road. When I look back, I know many of the events in my life were never contemplated in my wildest dreams. Although it is easier for us to make predictions about next week than next year, nothing is ever certain, because life can dish out surprises that seem to come out of nowhere. It would be wonderful, I mused, if we were allowed to peek into the future on occasion.

According to Albert, however, the future is just an illusion found on Earth, where we see time as a linear progression from past to present to future. Albert had explained that on the Spirit Side there is no past or future, only the present—and everything that has happened in the "past" or that will happen in the "future" is all happening now in the present. I found this concept difficult to understand because I was so conditioned to viewing time in a linear fashion.

Since everyone on Earth is stuck with the illusion of linear time, which seems very real to us, I was curious to find out if it was possible for someone to peer into our linear future to see what might transpire. I was aware of psychics with precognitive abilities who predict future events for their clients, although I wondered if these predictions were truly etched in stone with no possibility of change. I suspected the answer to this question would not be found on the Internet or in any library, so I decided to ask Albert for his thoughts about the future.

Albert did not disappoint as he provided his thoughtful response: "As I mentioned to you before, the idea that linear time is an illusion is a very difficult concept for humans to grasp, even though it is crystal clear to the souls on the Spirit Side. You will understand this reality when you transition back to the Spirit Side, but in the meantime let me give you a simple analogy to help you comprehend."

"Imagine you are standing in front of a forest that has one path leading into the dense thicket of trees. Inside this forest is a labyrinth of paths that branch out from the first path into an elaborate network of trails that meander through the trees. Ultimately, all the walkways exit into a broad meadow on the other side of the forest. But unlike some labyrinths that exist on Earth, the maze in this forest does not have any dead ends—all paths exit into the meadow despite all the twists and turns along the way. In other words, it is not possible to become lost or trapped in this maze; you will always find an exit that leads to the meadow.

"This is similar to your life on Earth. When you were born, you were standing in front of the only path into the forest. Even though you were just beginning your life when you took your first tentative steps into the forest, all of the many branches from the path already existed, and all the possible scenarios for your future were already in place. Thus your 'future' already existed in your 'present.' As your life proceeded, you had to choose which path to take whenever you came to a fork in the road. Your journey through the forest would have been different for each branch of the trail because you would have encountered unique people, places, and events on every path.

"Before you were born, you prepared a Life Plan for your life on Earth, which was designed to allow you to experience and learn the things you needed for your evolution as a soul. Your Life Plan sketched out a path for you through the forest that would allow you to achieve your goals. Because you are not allowed to remember what you put in your Life Plan, and you have free will to make decisions, there is no assurance you will follow the most desirable path through the forest. You are not left to flounder blindly in this maze, however, since you have several spirit guides who send you messages about which way to go at every crossroad you encounter. These messages, which come to you as intuitive thoughts, gut feelings, and coincidental events, are very subtle and can be easily missed or misunderstood.

"Furthermore, the maze of paths has many interconnections so you will always be able to get back on track even if you have taken a few wrong turns. And no matter which route you end up taking to the finish line for your life, you will always experience things that are useful in some way for your evolution. No journey through the forest is ever wasted or unfruitful; each will provide you with opportunities for growth.

"The good news is that no matter which paths you choose as you live your life, you will always emerge from the forest into the meadow on the other side. In this analogy, as you likely have guessed, the meadow on the other side of the forest is the Spirit Side, where you will always return after each incarnation no matter which route you took during your life."

Albert's explanation made sense to me, but I sought confirmation that I really understood the concept. So I ventured forth with my take on his analogy: "So when I was born, I was standing in front of the forest at the only entry point, and all the possible scenarios for my future existed in all the branches of the maze that were already in place. And one of these routes through the forest would be actualized as my life path after I began my journey and traveled through the woodland to the meadow. The people, places, and events I encounter on my journey will depend on where I focus my attention by choosing my passage through the forest. And all the other paths still exist, even though I did not experience what they had to offer."

"I think you are beginning to grasp the basics of what I have told you," Albert conceded. "Remember, though, you are struggling with a concept that is not easily assimilated by your human mind with its many limitations. It is not essential for you to fully understand this paradigm during your journey on Earth. Your understanding, or lack thereof, will not have any noticeable effect on the rest of your life. So do not spend much time trying to wrap your mind around this concept. Your time will be better spent focusing on listening to the messages from your guides so you can live the life you had planned before you were born."

"Is it possible, Albert, for a psychic with precognitive abilities to predict events in my future?"

"The short answer, like Yogi Berra observed, is that predictions are hard to make, especially about the future. And this is even more difficult now that 'the future ain't what it used to be.'"

"But setting aside the frivolity for the moment, I can confirm there are many psychics who can tap into spirits beyond the veil to predict the future; however, these predictions are not etched in stone. What they foresee are the events most likely to happen, assuming that all the factors present when the predictions are made continue in the normal course. For example, if a psychic predicts you will be awarded the promotion you have been hoping for, it is assumed you will continue to be diligent and productive right up to the time of your promotion. If, however, you slack off and relax after hearing that you will win the promotion, the prediction will not come true because you changed one of the important factors in your life.

"Another possibility is that the free-will actions of someone else could derail the predicated outcome. Maybe your boss will be transferred to another department and your new boss will not appreciate your contributions as much as your old boss. This could result in another person getting the promotion.

"Predictions like these are not intended to cause major changes in your life practices, since that would be self-defeating. In the example I just gave you, the prediction that you would win the promotion was intended to stop you from worrying about the outcome and save you from more sleepless nights and grouchy days. As long as you stayed the course, you would win the promotion, and the intervening time would be much more enjoyable.

"Sometimes these predictions are designed to spur you to make a change in your life. You might be told that you will suffer major health problems unless you start to exercise regularly and eat healthful food. This would be a message for you to change your lifestyle in order to avoid a heart attack down the road."

"Is it possible," I wondered, "for someone on the Spirit Side to actually see what the future holds for me, a prediction not based on assumptions and probability?"

"There are advanced souls on the Spirit Side who can see the actual outcome of a person's life on Earth. These are souls who have completed their incarnations on Earth and who have evolved to a higher level. But the spirits who communicate with the psychics do not have access to this information, or, if they do, they are not allowed to convey this information to people on Earth or to other souls who are still incarnating on the Earth plane. Thus your soul and your guides were not privy to this information when you were devising your Life Plan.

"Likewise, if you were allowed to see the final outcome of your life after you were born, it would affect your free-will decisions and the path you might otherwise take."

"Is it possible," I continued, "to travel back to the past or forward to the future?"

"You can't travel back to the past and interact with people or things in a physical way, although you can observe events from the past by accessing the Akashic Records. As you have seen, these records allow you to view what happened in your previous lives as well as the lives of anyone else you are curious about. You can view these past lives as an observer only, and you cannot physically intervene or change anything that has already happened.

"It is not possible for you to travel to the future in a physical sense, nor can you access the records of future events in your present stage of evolution. Only very advanced spirits, who no longer need to incarnate on the denser planes, are allowed to peer into the immutable future."

I was not surprised by Albert's response, since our free-will decisions would not really be free if we were burdened with knowledge of future events. And as Albert often reminded me, there was no point dwelling on the future. So I decided to change the topic and ask Albert for information about where he fit into the scheme of things. Was he an angel or a Master? Did he have a special role to fulfill?

Chapter 16

Who Is Albert?

Albert has been a very significant influence in my life since the day I first met him in 2007. Since then, he disclosed to me many revelations that were startling, comforting, inspiring, and often mind-boggling. Albert was always full of surprises, and I could never anticipate what he might tell me next.

And I never fully understood who he was. He told he was a soul like all other souls and one of my spirit guides. And he admitted at one point that he and I had lived together in several previous lives on Earth. Other than that, I did not know much about him. Albert never talked about himself unless I asked him a direct question, which he would answer only if he felt it was something I needed to know at the time.

Despite his previous reluctance to talk about himself, my curiosity got the better of me, and I prodded Albert for more information. He reluctantly told me he had accepted a special assignment from the Council of Wise Ones because he felt an obligation to help in any way he could.

His assignment was to be a special messenger for the Council on Earth. He was one of the souls selected to communicate with humans in unusual ways to disseminate the missives from the Council. Albert confirmed he had graduated from the Earth school and no longer needed to incarnate on this planet, and his new mission was to use the wisdom he had gained from his own lives on Earth to help humans make the shift. Albert reiterated that he did not like to use labels, so he would not confirm or deny he was a Master or another type of special spirit.

It was because of his special assignment that he appeared to me as the homeless man, and his conversations with me during the writing of *Dancing on a Stamp* were designed to promulgate the messages from the Council. It was hoped these revelations would prod humans to take their first tentative steps on the path to higher consciousness. And his rendezvous with me on the street that day had been planned before I was born, even though I did not remember it. I had been chosen as one of his messengers because I had lived previous lives as an author, and he expected that some of these residual writing skills might leak through to my current life. Albert confirmed that I had a duty to broadcast his truths to the multitudes and that any resistance would be futile—since Spirit will always win the day, one way or another.

So even though I still did not know much more about Albert and his status on the Spirit Side, I wondered if he could tell me if there was a hierarchy of souls, with more advanced souls being superior to those who were further down the evolutionary ladder.

When I raised the question with Albert, he told me all souls are considered equal because they are all part of the Source. The souls that have evolved to a higher state are not better than or superior to other souls, much like a student in high school is not considered to be better than a child in kindergarten.

The more advanced souls are able assist other souls with their evolution, and this gives them special recognition from everyone in the spirit realm. These highly evolved souls do not consider themselves to be superior to others, nor do they expect praise or homage. They are humble and loving spirits who enjoy helping other souls grow and evolve, and they do not want special treatment.

Albert conceded, however, that it was useful for some purposes to slot souls into different categories to help the Council of Wise Ones organize and supervise incarnations on the denser planes. He did his best to describe these categories as simply as possible, without detracting from the overriding principle that all spirits are equal in the eyes of the Source.

"At the first level are the souls that have recently spun out from the Source to begin their evolution by exploring all that the Source has created. These souls left the absolute love and security of the Source to experience life in the denser planes of the Universe. They have traveled throughout the galaxies searching for planets with interesting and challenging life forms that would be good vehicles for incarnation. They are still in the process of experiencing the things and learning the lessons they need for their growth, and they will continue to incarnate until they have 'graduated' from life on the denser planes.

"Souls do not learn and evolve at the same rate, and there are no deadlines for the completion of their journeys. All souls can choose their own pace for growth, and there is never any jealousy or envy when some souls evolve faster than others.

"The next evolutionary level consists of souls that have incarnated on the denser planes numerous times, gaining wisdom from their many lives on difficult planets like Earth. When they are on the Spirit Side, they will often act as spirit guides for other souls since their own experiences on the denser planes will be very helpful when they provide guidance to the souls they are coaching. They will often volunteer to fill roles on Earth needed by other souls—even when it will not contribute much to their own evolution.

"Then there are the Masters—highly evolved souls who no longer need to incarnate on the denser planes. These souls have frequently incarnated on Earth to play significant roles in human development. Jesus Christ, Buddha, Mohamed, and Moses are well-known examples, while many other Masters have roamed Earth over the centuries quietly making significant contributions to human civilization. And there are many Masters on Earth today helping humans expand their consciousness. The Masters who remain on the Spirit Side help other souls evolve by freely sharing their wisdom in lectures and seminars.

"The Wise Ones are also highly evolved souls who serve on the various Councils that oversee incarnations on the denser planes. They use their wisdom to assist souls develop Life Plans that are suitable to achieve the life experiences needed for their growth, and they help returning souls analyze and understand the lives they have just finished.

"In their own unique category are the angels. These special spirits usually do not incarnate into physical bodies on Earth since they were highly evolved when they spun out from the Source. Their labor of love is to help humans with their struggles on Earth. Some of them function as guardian angels to ensure that humans do not die accidently before their souls are ready to exit their incarnations. And sometimes they will appear on Earth as physical entities to provide guidance, inspiration, and hope when it is needed. Whenever a soul is temporarily lost after its physical death, they will lead it back to the Spirit Side where it can continue its evolution.

"The most important thing to remember, however, is that all souls and spirits are equal in every sense no matter which category they are in, and all are happy to contribute to the evolution of all other souls in whatever way they can."

Despite my prodding, Albert would not reveal where I was on the evolutionary ladder. I sensed that I wasn't a Master, but I didn't know if I was a newcomer to the Earth plane or an old soul. Albert said this information would distract me from the goals I needed to achieve, so he declined to comment, and his poker face did not provide any clues.

I noted that his explanation about the stages of soul evolution did not make any reference to the Source. I reflected on what Albert had told me about the Source in our earlier conversations as I resolved to pump Albert for more information about the Creator.

Chapter 17

The Source

Previously, Albert had revealed that the Source is the creator of everything in Universe and that all things in the Universe—all the galaxies, stars, planets, and life forms—are connected to one another and to the Source, which is the sum total of everything that exists. This concept of God was quite different from the Roman Catholic version I was taught as a child. The Catholic Church believed that God was the Supreme Being who manipulated and controlled everything on Earth. According to the Church, God created all humans and sent them to Earth to serve his purpose. God made rules for us to follow (which were revealed to us by the Church), and he demanded respectful worship and adoration from everyone. And after we died, we would appear before God to receive his judgment. If we had paid proper homage to him and had followed his rules, we would be allowed to enter Heaven. But if we had broken his rules without making amends we would be punished in Hell for eternity. God was like a king sitting on a gold throne dispensing rewards or punishment to the souls who had finished their lives on Earth. In the eyes of the Church, it would be outrageous blasphemy for humans to consider themselves to be part of God.

The Church's version of God bestowed him with several negative human attributes. He was vain because he demanded to be worshiped by humans in special ways and vengeful if we didn't follow his rules. He gave humans free will to act on Earth even though it meant that many of his rules would be broken. God would be a loving and forgiving deity to those people who stayed on the straight and narrow, but cold and heartless to everyone else.

In the Church's view, God manipulated all the events in your life and orchestrated all the good things and bad things that happened to you and your loved ones. If you enjoyed good fortune, you were supposed to thank God for his generosity, and if you experienced adversity it was because God had decided to make you suffer. You were not supposed to know the reasons for the good fortune or the bad luck; you were expected to accept whatever God dished out to you without question since, according to the Church, "God works in mysterious ways."

The Christian God was a divine being who expected to be feared by humans. It was considered a compliment, an indication you were a good Christian, if you were labeled as a "God-fearing" person. You were supposed to fear God because he had the power to punish you for your misdeeds, and you should be afraid of offending him in any way.

I came to realize later in my life that the Christian God was really an anthropomorphic deity created by the holy men of the Church to help them control the masses through guilt and fear. They gave their God the attributes of a despot on Earth since that was something they could easily sell to their followers. Thus, like a king or queen on Earth, the Christian God expected his followers to pay homage to him and obey his commands, failing which he would become angry and vengeful. The early leaders of the Church knew that a God with these characteristics would serve them well in their quest to control their followers.

As I revealed in *Dancing on a Stamp*, Albert rejected the Christian version of God as the creative fiction of a few misguided holy men. Albert unequivocally dispelled the notion that the Source is a vain and vengeful deity that makes rules and hands out punishment to the miscreants on Earth. The Source is not a separate divine being that is aloof and superior to all other beings. Instead, everyone and everything are part of the Source, which is the totality of everything in the Universe. The Source is the genesis and embodiment of all love in the Universe.

Although I understood Albert's description of the Source, it was difficult for me to truly grasp the idea that we are all part of the

Source. It was a radical concept when compared to the Christian version of God.

So I asked Albert if he could take me to the Source. Albert nodded his agreement, and we flew east over the North American continent and across the Atlantic Ocean, touching down in Hyde Park, London, where the late morning sun was shining brightly.

Albert pointed to a tall majestic oak tree and began: "That beautiful tree over there is an aspect of the Source. The squirrel sitting on one of its branches is also an aspect of the Source. The water fountain beside the tree is another facet of the Source, as are the sun, the clouds, and the birds flying overhead. The smiling face of the little girl feeding the pigeons is an aspect of the Source. The Source has many faces, and you will always be surrounded by the Source wherever you are, because everything in your world—all the people, creatures, and plants, as well as the mountains, oceans, and glaciers—are all individual aspects of the Source. Whenever you open your eyes you will see the Source."

"Does the Source have a central focal point, a place where all of its aspects originated?" I responded.

"I can take you to the hub of the Source, the starting point for everything created by the Source, which is sometimes referred to as the Central Sun. This is where you began your journey of exploration long ago as a spark of energy. We can stay only for a little while because you still have a lot to do on Earth."

Albert led me up to our assembly point high above Earth and pointed toward the stars. The stars disappeared for a few seconds until we emerged from the blackness, hovering above a brilliant orb floating in space. It looked like our sun, only much brighter. As we moved closer, this scintillating ball of light loomed larger and larger until it completely filled my field of vision. Although the light from this orb was exceedingly bright, it did not hurt my eyes, and I did not feel any excess heat—only pleasant warmth.

After entering this magnificent globe, we were totally surrounded by soft light and immersed in a wonderful feeling of love, peace, and security. It was similar to the feeling I had when I first encountered Albert as the homeless man, except this feeling was a thousand times more intense. I felt like I had merged with the center of all love in the Universe, the root of all happiness and joy in our cosmos. But I still retained my individuality—my memories and personality—even though I was immersed in this macrocosm of ecstasy. I sensed that this was where I had been spawned long ago as a being of energy. I felt totally at one with the Source and everything else that existed. It was the ultimate sense of unity.

I could have stayed there forever, except I knew my soul journey must continue. So I reluctantly followed Albert as he led me away from the Central Sun and back to Earth. I understood then that human words could not possibly describe the Source in any meaningful way.

Chapter 18

Keep on Dancing

It was another Sunday night, as I lay in bed staring at the ceiling. Tomorrow would bring another Monday morning, followed by all the other days of the week until once again I would be gazing at my ceiling on a Sunday night. At times the cycle of the week seemed endless and never-changing, although I understood this was an illusion amplified by my distorted focus on the passage of time. In fact, everything in the Universe is in a constant state of change, even if many of the changes are imperceptible to humans on this planet.

I smiled with satisfaction as I reflected on my recent adventures with Albert. He had been quite a tour guide—showing me many breathtaking vistas and extraordinary life forms. And on every trip he had shared his wisdom with insightful revelations, while demonstrating the magic of love and compassion.

After my visits to the Spirit Side, life on Earth seemed rather tedious and uneventful. But I understood that life on this planet was not intended to be a blissful adventure free of adversity. I had carefully planned my life to experience the things, both good and bad, I needed for my evolution, although the reasons were not apparent to me now. I had to assume, to paraphrase Shakespeare, that there had been method to my madness.

I did not know how closely I had been able to follow my Life Plan to this point; however, I knew what I did in the past should not dictate my path for the future. Every morning was the beginning of the rest of my life, and my challenge was to choose the best route from this point forward. Albert had provided me with sage guidance from the spirit realm during our time together, and now it was up to me to put the plan into action.

The last time I saw Albert he had hinted that his nightly visits would soon be put on hold so I could focus on writing my book, and I dearly wanted to wring a few more nuggets of wisdom from him before he disappeared.

When Albert reappeared later that night, he confirmed that our adventures had come to an end for the time being so I could finish my manuscript. I frowned and shrugged my shoulders in resignation even though his announcement was no surprise.

"Before you go, Albert, do you have any parting words for me?"

Albert had been expecting this, so he was ready with his response. "You must remind yourself everyday about the nature of your journey and who you really are. You view life too seriously and you need to lighten up and enjoy your sojourn on Earth. Try to see the humor in the world around you and laugh at your foibles and the antics of your fellow humans, just as we do in the spirit realm. Nothing that happens on Earth continues after death, and the only things you will take with you are the memories of your life and the wisdom you gleaned from your experiences.

"Remember to reach out to touch the Source every day. Pause often to hug your wife and kids, to cradle your granddaughter in your arms, and give your little dog a few pats. Smile at strangers you pass on the street, and be generous to the homeless people asking for handouts, because they are all souls who are connected to you and to one another as individual aspects of the Source. Let your actions display the compassion that all humans should feel for one another and for the other creatures on your planet.

"Forgive those who step on your toes because, like you, they are still learning about the dance of life on Earth. Don't waste your energy comparing yourself to other people because you are all distinct aspects of the Source experiencing a human journey designed to fulfill your requirements for wisdom and growth. Since every soul has mapped out its own unique path for evolution, you should respect the life choices made by others with understanding and compassion. And never make judgments about other people because you do not know where they have been or where they are going.

"Respect all other creatures living on Earth because they too are individual aspects of the Source who incarnated on your planet to experience what it has to offer. Treat them with dignity and kindness and do your best to halt the abuse heaped on them by other humans. Lead by example whenever you encounter the critters that share your planet, and be willing to step up to the plate whenever necessary to stop their suffering.

"Honor Mother Earth for all the gifts she provides to you each and every day. Make sure you are not contributing to the pollution of your beautiful planet, and speak out forcefully whenever possible to implore your fellow humans to stop abusing your environment.

"And remember to embrace all other humans with love and compassion and treat everyone the way you would like to be treated yourself. Discard your illusions of separation and acknowledge every day that you are all connected to one another and to the Source. Be part of the crusade to distribute the bounty we harvest from Mother Earth to all people on your planet, regardless of where they live, the color of their skin, or the God they worship.

"You are an eternal spirit having a human journey in a life you chose for yourself, and you are the creator of your own reality. Choose hope instead of fear, love and not hate, and happiness over despair, and your time on Earth will be much more rewarding. Death should not be feared because it is merely a doorway leading you back Home to the warm embrace of your loved ones. So relax, enjoy your adventure, and relish all your life experiences, because you cannot become lost no matter which path you follow.

"And stop rushing through life like you are running a sprint. You are on a journey that has no timetable and no finish line, so slow down and experience life to the fullest. Do not be afraid to break out of your comfort zone and try different things because failure is not an option, and you will grow and evolve from every new experience. And don't be concerned about what other people think of you because it is your journey to enjoy, not theirs.

"Think back to the ballroom I described to you when you were writing your first book. Remember the elegant dance hall with stained-glass windows and gleaming hardwood floors, with the band playing an enchanting waltz that had everyone whirling around the room in a dance of joy. But you were stuck to the same spot like you were dancing on a stamp.

"After a few nudges from me, you finally broke free from your shackles to join the frolic. Now I want you to take the next step.

"Walk out of the ballroom and stand by the shore of the placid lake in front of the dance hall. Look at the full moon hovering above the horizon, and follow the moonbeam across the water to the edge of the shore. Now kick off our shoes and step onto this path of light shimmering on the lake. Take a few more steps and feel the tingling photons of the light beam on your feet. Keep walking for a hundred paces, then turn around and look back. You can see the lights from the dance hall shining through the stained-glass windows and hear the music wafting up into the night sky.

"But the music has changed—now it is a lively Celtic tune played by a merry band of fiddlers. Now cast your mind back to your childhood when you were five. Remember that Sunday evening when you bounced merrily in your chair to the sound of a toe-tapping Irish jig served up by Uncle Jim and his fiddle, with Uncle Joe on the piano. And then you jumped up and danced all by yourself with the carefree exuberance of youth. You didn't know how to dance—you made up the steps as you went—but you did not care as long as you could move your arms and legs in a rhythmic rapture of joy.

"Now listen to the music streaming from the ballroom and feel it resonate through your body. Move your arms and legs in sync with the lively tempo of the band, and dance like you did when you were five. When your dance on Earth is over, you will follow the moonbeam Home to join the other merry souls who are dancing forever with Spirit.

Albert's eyes were sparkling like never before, and his infectious smile gleamed brightly as he wrapped his arms around me in a warm embrace. Then with a wink and a wave, he disappeared into the night sky.

About The Author

Garnet Schulhauser is a retired lawyer who lives near Victoria, on Vancouver Island, with his wife, Cathy, and little dog, Abby. He grew up on a small farm in Saskatchewan and moved to Calgary, Canada, after law school where he practiced corporate law for over thirty years with two blue-chip law firms. After retiring from his law firm in 2008, he began his new career as an author and his first book, *Dancing on a Stamp*, was published in 2012. Since the release of his first book, Garnet has been active with book signing tours and speaking engagements and has been a frequent guest on radio talk shows. When he is not writing or connecting with his followers, Garnet enjoys golfing, nature walks in the forest with Abby, and family gatherings with his sons, Blake and Colin, and their partners, Lauren and Bergis, and granddaughter Kymera.

In *Dancing on a Stamp*, Garnet recounts how his life changed dramatically one day in 2007 (while still practicing law) when he was confronted on the street by a homeless man named Albert (who was actually a wise spirit in disguise—an emissary from the spirit world). This seemingly chance encounter launched a provocative dialogue with Albert who disclosed startling new truths about all of life's big questions, including our true nature as eternal souls, the cycle of reincarnation on Earth, and how we create our own reality through free-will choices. He wrote **Dancing on a Stamp** at Albert's request so that these revelations would be available to everyone.

Garnet's second book, **Dancing Forever with Spirit**, describes his most recent adventures with Albert who appeared in his bedroom room one night to guide him on a series of out-of-body adventures to explore the wonders of the Universe, including the Akashic Records, distant planets with fascinating life forms, and a human civilization that made the shift to the New Earth. Albert's goal was to encourage humans to stop their abuse of Mother Earth and all of her inhabitants by casting aside their negative emotions and in favor of love and compassion.

Other Books By Ozark Mountain Publishing, Inc.

Dolores Cannon
A Soul Remembers Hiroshima
Between Death and Life
Conversations with Nostradamus,
　　Volume I, II, III
The Convoluted Universe -Book One,
　　Two, Three, Four
The Custodians
Five Lives Remembered
Jesus and the Essenes
Keepers of the Garden
Legacy from the Stars
The Legend of Starcrash
The Search for Hidden Sacred Knowledge
They Walked with Jesus
The Three Waves of Volunteers and the
　　New Earth
Aron Abrahamsen
Holiday in Heaven
Out of the Archives – Earth Changes
Justine Alessi & M. E. McMillan
Rebirth of the Oracle
Kathryn/Patrick Andries
Naked In Public
Kathryn Andries
Dream Doctor
Soul Choices: Six Paths to Find Your Life
　　Purpose
Soul Choices: Six Paths to Fulfilling
　　Relationships
Tom Arbino
You Were Destined to be Together
Rev. Keith Bender
The Despiritualized Church
O.T. Bonnett, M.D./Greg Satre
Reincarnation: The View from Eternity
What I Learned After Medical School
Why Healing Happens
Julia Cannon
Soul Speak – The Language of Your Body
Ronald Chapman
Seeing True
Albert Cheung
The Emperor's Stargate
Jack Churchward
Lifting the Veil on the Lost Continent of Mu
The Stone Tablets of Mu
Sherri Cortland
Guide Group Fridays
Raising Our Vibrations for the New Age
Spiritual Tool Box
Windows of Opportunity

Cinnamon Crow
Chakra Zodiac Healing Oracle
Teen Oracle
Michael Dennis
Morning Coffee with God
God's Many Mansions
Claire Doyle Beland
Luck Doesn't Happen by Chance
Jodi Felice
The Enchanted Garden
Max Flindt/Otto Binder
Mankind: Children of the Stars
Arun & Sunanda Gandhi
The Forgotten Woman
Maiya & Geoff Gray-Cobb
Angels -The Guardians of Your Destiny
Seeds of the Soul
Julia Hanson
Awakening To Your Creation
Donald L. Hicks
The Divinity Factor
Anita Holmes
Twidders
Antoinette Lee Howard
Journey Through Fear
Vara Humphreys
The Science of Knowledge
Victoria Hunt
Kiss the Wind
James H. Kent
Past Life Memories As A Confederate
　　Soldier
Mandeep Khera
Why?
Dorothy Leon
Is Jehovah An E.T
Mary Letorney
Discover The Universe Within You
Sture Lönnerstrand
I Have Lived Before
Irene Lucas
Thirty Miracles in Thirty Days
Susan Mack & Natalia Krawetz
My Teachers Wear Fur Coats
Patrick McNamara
Beauty and the Priest
Maureen McGill & Nola Davis
Live From the Other Side
Henry Michaelson
And Jesus Said – A Conversation
Dennis Milner
Kosmos

For more information about any of the above titles, soon to be released titles,
or other items in our catalog, write or visit our website:
PO Box 754, Huntsville, AR 72740
www.ozarkmt.com

Other Books By Ozark Mountain Publishing, Inc.

Guy Needler
Avoiding Karma
Beyond the Source – Book 1, Book 2
The History of God
Sherry O'Brian
Peaks and Valleys
Riet Okken
The Liberating Power of Emotions
John Panella
The Gnostic Papers
Victor Parachin
Sit a Bit
Nikki Pattillo
A Spiritual Evolution
Children of the Stars
Rev. Grant H. Pealer
A Funny Thing Happened on the
    Way to Heaven
Worlds Beyond Death
Karen Peebles
The Other Side of Suicide
Victoria Pendragon
Sleep Magic
Walter Pullen
Evolution of the Spirit
Christine Ramos, RN
A Journey Into Being
Debra Rayburn
Let's Get Natural With Herbs
Charmian Redwood
Coming Home to Lemuria
David Rivinus
Always Dreaming
Briceida Ryan
The Ultimate Dictionary of Dream
    Language

M. Don Schorn
Elder Gods of Antiquity
Legacy of the Elder Gods
Gardens of the Elder Gods
Reincarnation...Stepping Stones of Life
Garnet Schulhauser
Dancing on a Stamp
Annie Stillwater Gray
Education of a Guardian Angel
Blair Styra
Don't Change the Channel
Natalie Sudman
Application of Impossible Things
Dee Wallace/Jarrad Hewett
The Big E
Dee Wallace
Conscious Creation
James Wawro
Ask Your Inner Voice
Janie Wells
Payment for Passage
Dennis Wheatley/ Maria Wheatley
The Essential Dowsing Guide
Jacquelyn Wiersma
The Zodiac Recipe
Sherry Wilde
The Forgotten Promise
Stuart Wilson & Joanna Prentis
Atlantis and the New Consciousness
Beyond Limitations
The Essenes -Children of the Light
The Magdalene Version
Power of the Magdalene
Robert Winterhalter
The Healing Christ

For more information about any of the above titles, soon to be released titles,
or other items in our catalog, write or visit our website:
PO Box 754, Huntsville, AR 72740
www.ozarkmt.com